THE SEVEN INTENTIONS OF MOURNING

Carrying the Cross of Grief, with Meaning and Hope

John O'Shaughnessy
with Sandy O'Shaughnessy

lectio

Lectio Publishing, LLC
Hobe Sound, Florida, USA

www.lectiopublishing.com

Software System –

Morning/end - Check kids in & out of
camp, working in office, parent questions
documents, computer work
€17.74&19.74   10,104
1:30/8 - 4:00/4:30pm
$19 - $20   Salary

Chapter Three was authored by Sandy O'Shaughnessy; all other chapters were authored by John O'Shaughnessy.

ISBN 978-1-943901-10-4
Library of Congress Control Number: 2018967517

Published by Lectio Publishing, LLC
Hobe Sound, Florida 33455
www.lectiopublishing.com

For David John Prebenda and Ann Catherine O'Shaughnessy,
you were an inspiration in life
and are a source of boundless love in eternal life.
We do what we do to honor each of you,
and all we have loved and lost.

And for all those who mourn.
We hope and pray you find these words helpful
as you begin to build your bridge
that leads you into a new and different life.

Foreword

If we are blessed with stories of love, we will grieve when the story concludes, but the love lives on.

This book is both personal and professional. The personal led to the professional. In 1998, my first wife Ann, died after a 36-month struggle with lung cancer. She was 42 years old. I was 41 with two young boys. I was a corporate guy then. Driven, some would say. We all watched almost helplessly as a wife, a mother, a daughter, a sister and a friend slowly succumbed to this dreadful disease. It was painful. When death came it was, in a sense, a blessing. But now what? I was an "only parent" to Eric and Collin who were all of twelve and ten at the time. I had little idea what to do. But I knew then that this experience had changed me in a profound way and forever.

About the same time that Ann was dying, worlds apart, Sandy and her first husband David, were entering their journey. For about two years David battled Ewing's Sarcoma, a particularly rare yet deadly form of cancer. And during her struggle with David, raising two young children, Sandy's mother was in a car accident and became paralyzed from the C2 vertebra down. Now Sandy had two battles to contend with. Her mother died in 1999. David died in 2000; he was only 35. Sandy too became an only parent to two young children, Morgan and Ryan, who were six and three. She too had little idea what to do. She too knew this experience had changed her forever.

Yes, Sandy and I were fortunate. We met, we fell in love all over again, and we married. But this book isn't about our love story, it's about the ministry that formed because of our grief, our pain, and our suffering. It's about the many stories that grew from this ministry. It's about the meaning that was discovered years after our hearts were broken. Meaning that wasn't understood amid our mourning, and only later revealed in a mission to help others heal from the devastating wounds of losing a loved one.

Anointed

It was early December in 2010, the beginning of Advent, during Eucharistic Adoration, when I heard these words—Catholic Bereavement Ministry. Where these words came from and how I heard them is a great mystery. Or is it? I had been working in bereavement with a local nonprofit, Christian-based organization. The idea that Catholics needed any special help had never entered my mind. So I can only conclude that these words were divinely sent from the Holy Spirit. A few weeks after Christmas I was talking to our pastor, Fr. John Riccardo, who encouraged me to act upon this request, mostly because who it came from, but partly because of the need for a faith-based Catholic bereavement ministry.

Good Mourning Ministry

In the spring of 2011, two years after we married, Sandy and I began Good Mourning Ministry, a Catholic bereavement apostolate. The model we introduced was simple. The workshops are prayerful, practical and personal. We spend about one-third of our time in church, with a priest or deacon guiding us through our faith. We spend time in prayer, in song mostly before the Blessed Sacrament, the Body of Christ.

It's practical too. We educate the participants about what grief is and what mourning is, and what they are not. It's deeply personal, as the participants spend time in small "Grief Peer Groups" where they can share their stories in a safe, affirming and validating environment. All loss is unique, but these groups are formed based on similar types of loss as well as relative ages.

Grieving with Great Hope

By that fall we facilitated our first "Grieving with Great Hope" workshop. About 35 people pre-registered. We were thrilled that so many people were trusting us to help support them on their grief journey. But then another 45 showed up that night. 80 people is a large grief workshop. "Have faith," we thought. The Holy Spirit will guide.

Since then, not to mention the DVD Series that we produced, over 100 "Grieving with Great Hope" workshops have been held at Catholic Parishes across the country, with over 3,000 participants. About half of all participants who attend our workshop have lost a spouse.

This group tends to be older, however at our first workshop there was a group of widows and one widower in their 30s and 40s. The cause of death is often split between a sudden death and a long illness. Another large group are parents who have lost a child. This almost always represents a sudden loss, either by an accident, completed suicide or a drug or alcohol overdose. The other remaining large group is of children who have lost one or both parents. And of course, there are other losses, siblings and friends and the like.

These grieving people tell stories. About the power of love, and how it endures the crush of death. About the power of hope and how it meets us along the journey of grief, guiding us to a new and different life. About the gift of faith and the comfort it brings. We have seen transformations in people. We have seen solidarity amongst people. We have witnessed people dealing with tragic losses who found light amidst the darkness. We have seen people make mission.

This book is not only dedicated to these people who took an active approach with their grief, it is about them too. Over the years, and at almost every workshop, we have picked up stories. Some of these stories find their way into subsequent workshops. Some of these stories have been woven into this book. The names, if mentioned, have been changed to protect the identities. It is our hope, that these stories will help those reading them.

The Fruit

"I am the true vine, and my Father is the vine grower. He takes away every branch in me that does not bear fruit, and every one that does he prunes so that it bears more fruit" (John 15:1). We have learned a great deal over the last few years. The participants who have attended our workshops seem to be generally resilient. That despite their loss or losses, they have found ways to move forward with hope. The process isn't easy, it's painful, but when we face our pain, we diminish its effect on us. When we realize that there are intentional things we can do, we begin to take back control of our lives.

It takes courage to come to one of these workshops. For many, they are coming to a foreign place, meeting new people, all while grieving. The first session or two can be difficult. But we notice every time, with each subsequent session, a distinct increase in the noise level. People start talking about their story, they open-up about what is going on in their life, and how they feel. It's powerful medicine. By the closing session, many times, strangers have become friends and the healing continues after the workshop, in a coffee shop or breaking bread at a dinner table.

We have not created new ways to grieve. We have adapted some previous concepts we believe are efficacious, and molded them into an "Intention-Oriented, faith-based" approach. We have however given mourning a fresh look, a new lens to look through that looks outward, away from ourselves and toward something or someone else. Towards more of a mission of healing. But perhaps more importantly, we simply create an environment that is validating, compassionate, nurturing and educational, where the Holy Spirit is welcomed, and in which, the participants become to each other, disciples of hope. We are witnesses, that mourning with great intention, is a powerful way to respond to loss. Where we "Bear one another's burdens, and so fulfill the law of Christ" (GAL 6:2).

After every workshop, we ask participants to fill out an evaluation. We have used the comments from these evaluations to make some subtle and not so subtle changes to the workshop. For instance, the earlier workshops were four-week, but the participants kept telling us it wasn't long enough. Some still tell us that, even after we extended it to five weeks. Others told us the time in grief peer groups wasn't long enough. So, we made some modifications to the format that allows for some more time for discussion.

Here is an average of how about 1,000 participants rated the workshop:

- Overall rating: excellent or very good — 96%
- Meet expectations: completely or mostly — 97%
- Would recommend to others — 99%

Some of the things that participants like the most:

- I know where I am in the mourning process.
- I like sharing my story with other people.
- I know it's healthy to mourn.
- I know it's good to laugh and cry.
- I know I am not alone.

- Faith will keep me strong.
- The Seven Intentions of Mourning are helpful.
- Learning about internal monologue.
- Learning about grief and mourning.

A few of the many testimonials:

- "I came in alone and left with new friends." Sandy Noland (Widow)
- "I came to this workshop completely lost. I was looking for direction. A path. This workshop really helped me do that." John Raasch (loss of Sister)
- "I found ways to acknowledge, express and share my thoughts and feelings with family and friends." Leon Debian (Widower)
- "I feel I have learned how to deal with the emotions I'm feeling and that there are steps I can take and things I can do that will help ease the pain when I feel hopeless. I think the Seven Intentions of Mourning will help bring healing." Rosanne Courtright (loss of Child)

How This Book is Written

This book was written largely because workshop participants asked for more information about each of The Seven Intentions of Mourning. This is not a typical grief book. It is not written for Academics. It is not heavy on theory about stages, phases or patterns of grief. It is written for grieving people, trying to understand all that has happened, and what they can do about the fact that someone they love has died. We will see that grief is a reaction that prompts an invitation. The grief reaction is just as important as the invitation. Calvary preceded the empty tomb. Without suffering there is no Easter, and without Easter, there is no invitation to heal our mortal wounds through the redemptive blood of Christ. But grief only invites us to respond. It is not a mandate. It is only when we accept the invitation that we can begin to heal and even grow from this experience. In some cases, we will find that healing comes when we reach beyond our own outstretched arms and embrace the outstretched arms of someone else. In other words, we heal by loving our neighbor as we love our self. When we save another soul, we save our own.

We do not pretend to be academic theologians trying to carve out any new twist on Church doctrine. That is way above our pay grade, but we do pose some thoughts worthy of clerical attention. This book simply challenges us all to ask the fundamental question: who is my neighbor? And in asking that question, it inevitably leads to another question: what can I do to help them? If we place ourselves in the role of the Good Samaritan on the road to Jericho, then everyone we encounter could be the person who needs our help, the person to whom we show love, the person to whom we are a disciple of hope. We are taking what it means to be a Christian and shaping that around how we should mourn. "And as you wish that men would do to you, do so to them" (LUKE 6:31). In helping others we help ourselves. For we cannot profit from the fruit of His sacrifice, without sacrificing our profits for the fruit that is His Kingdom, His Body.

This book is written much like the workshop, in a prayerful, practical and personal format. With each of the Seven Intentions of Mourning, we will begin with a short prayer, and then a scripture passage. The chapter itself will be the practical application of the intention. After each intention, we have three questions for you to reflect on. Then you can write your own intention. Each intention will conclude by asking you to consider one of the Works of Mercy as a way you can help someone else.

We ask for your active participation in this journey, as you begin to build your bridge to a new and different life.

— John O'Shaughnessy

 HENRI J.M. NOUWEN

Every time we make a decision to love someone, we open ourselves to great suffering, because those we most love, cause us not only great joy, but also great pain. The greatest pain comes from leaving...the pain of leaving can tear us apart. Still, if we want to avoid the suffering of leaving, we will never experience the joy of loving. And love is stronger than fear., life is stronger than death, hope is stronger than despair. We have to trust that the risk of loving is always worth taking.

CONTENTS

Our faith, more precious than gold,
must be tried as through fire.

Servant of God Dorothy Day

Elizabeth Ann Seton

The Patron Saint of Grief

E lizabeth Ann Seton (1774-1821) was the first American-born person to be canonized by the Roman Catholic Church. She is the Patron Saint of grief. She was only three years old when her mother died. Her father remarried and had five additional children with Elizabeth's stepmother, Charlotte Barclay. This marriage however ended in divorce, with Charlotte rejecting Elizabeth. In 1794, at age 19, Elizabeth married William Seton, a wealthy businessman. They had five children. In addition, grieving her mother's death, she also grieved the death of her husband from tuberculosis just nine years into their marriage. She also buried two of her five children, also from tuberculosis. "The accidents in life separate us from our dearest friends but let us not despair." About grief she said, 'God is like a looking glass in which souls see each other. The more we are united to Him by love, the nearer we are to those who belong to Him."

In 1809 she founded the Sisters of Charity. This charity continues to this day, operating schools, hospitals and social service centers across the country. "We must pray without ceasing, in every occurrence and employment of our lives, that prayer which is rather a habit of lifting up the heart to God as is a constant communion with Him."

Canonized in 1975 by Pope Paul VI, her feast day is January 4.

Elizabeth Ann Seton, pray for us.

Introduction

For the next few minutes, imagine this is you. You are on a journey, a grief journey, with a story that is distinctively you. You are on a path in the woods. Alone at first. At some point along your journey, the path you are on will diverge into two paths. It is here that you will stop and pause. It is here that you will decide on which path you will choose. But for now, you simply walk.

Your loved one died. It may have been after a long illness. Or maybe there was no warning at all, no time to prepare. You knew this person for much of your life, or even all your life. You may have had many years with them, or little time at all. They were special to you—in many ways. Pick some of these ways, and perhaps add some others. The way their smile captured your heart every day. Maybe you birthed them and raised them. You loved the way they hugged you every morning. Their laugh and sense of humor was contagious. They were thoughtful. You shared your faith together with your Sunday morning ten o'clock Mass ritual. You golfed together. You took long walks. You attended their sporting events with great zest. You looked forward to many things, teaching them to ride a bicycle, walking her down the aisle. You had hopes and dreams and plans.

You had your struggles too. But now, you look back on these times when life seemed so unfair and these memories ring hollow in the face of your grief.

Now, there are many days when you cry. There are times when you feel angry, like Jesus in the temple. You even feel guilty, but you can't understand why. There is a deep sense of sadness that you cannot extinguish. You miss this person so much. You miss dinners together. You miss vacations. You miss watching your favorite television shows. You miss morning coffee time when you would catch up on everything. You miss going to church and praying together. It's as if pieces of your past have been scattered along the path you now walk. The dreams you held, the plans you made, the memories you collected. Things you see but can no longer hold. But with every step you brush into them, and they remind you of the void that remains.

Was this your spouse? Was this your child? Was this your mother or father? A friend? It is someone you love. Do you want them back? Or are you at peace with how they died? Would you like a "do-over"? Would you like one more chance to tell them how much you love them?

So you walk. On a path. One foot in front of the other. Do you know where you are going? Maybe not. You feel compelled to move. This path you are on is unrecognizable. You think way too much. Your mind takes you places you don't want to go. The days turn into weeks. Weeks into months. You grieve. You walk. You wonder what keeps you going. Grace perhaps. Must be God's grace you think. You accept this. He holds you in His hands. But still you grieve. You suffer.

Weeks or months have passed, maybe a year, then suddenly an old friend you haven't seen in a while, comes out of nowhere. The friend finds you crying, bent over with your hands on your head.

The old friend approaches you and asks, "Why are you crying?"

You look up. "Someone I love died."

"I'm sorry. When did this happen?" the friend asks.

"A few weeks ago, a couple of months, a year or two. It seems like yesterday."

"You're still sad. Why are you still sad?"

"I miss him (or her)," you say. "I miss his touch. His voice. I miss how he was late for everything. I was always the one who made sure we were on time. And you know, I'd complain every time he made me wait. Now I know how senseless this was. Now I miss waiting for him, only he's never late anymore.

"I'm very sorry," your old friend says. "This must be so painful for you. I cannot relate to what you are going through, but I would like to help you. How can I help you?"

You are surprised. You can't recall the last time someone sincerely offered to help you. Was it after the funeral? Was it the last time you ran into someone at the grocery store? Did they ever stop by with that casserole they promised? You think so, but some things remain a blur.

"Would you walk with me?" you ask. "Wherever we are going. Would you walk with me? Would you pray with me? I like to pray early in the morning. It's me and Jesus. He is just waking up too and we share a cup of coffee together. I tell Him what's on my mind. Sometimes Mary joins us. I pray with both. Would you walk with me?"

"I will," the friend replies. "I'd be happy to."

And so, you walk in the woods. The path isn't clear. Twigs and rocks and old tree limbs are strewn upon the way. There is nothing level about this path. Sometimes there are steep climbs and other times, without warning, sharp descents. As you share your story to your old friend, feelings bubble up and over. You're surprised that you feel better after you cry. You let the tears pour forth. Weeks turn into months. Months turn into more months, maybe a year or two.

Then, whenever it is, you approach a fork in the path. You remember someone once told you, you'd reach a fork in the journey of your grief. You didn't know what they meant, but you pretended to. The two of you stop. Your friend takes your hand. You look to your left. You see the path looks much the same as the road you've been on. The path of grief. The path of pain and suffering. The path of unforgiveness, anger and guilt. The path where sadness seems as endless as the tears.

Then you turn slightly to your right. This path appears different. Down this path you see healing. Down this path you see hope and forgiveness. Down this path are intentional ways to mourn. No one walks alone on this path. Grief is shared and transformed. Where feelings are felt and not feared. Down this path you see a great cloud of witnesses, cheering you on to run the race, to persevere. Down this path is even laughter mixed with tears. Where memories are shared and enjoyed. Boundless compassion flows along this path. Meaning and purpose is found along this path. You see it. You feel it. You smile a smile of hope.

Your friend turns to you. "Which path will you choose?"

For the first time in a long time, the sweet sense of solace temporally fills up your body. You start walking down the long and winding path that never ends. Your friend follows you and soon others join.

Alissa Parker's daughter Emilie was killed at the Sandy Hook Elementary School shooting, "It's a universal story about finding the light in all the darkness in the world," she says. "Finding the light all around us was not always easy to see, but I realized it was there and that I had to let that light back into my life."[1] Sandy remarked during her journey, "this is when she crawled out from under her rock." The fork in the road is not a destination. But the fork is real. What it looks like and when we arrive there is different for all of us. But we all arrive at this fork, these two paths that diverge, and when we arrive, we must then make a choice as to where we will go next. From Viktor Frankl, "When we can no longer change the situation we are in, we are challenged to change ourselves."[2]

Grief is forced upon us. It's painful. It's not romantic. We react. We suffer. Mourning is that clarion call in which we hear a challenge to respond. To behave in a way our loved ones would admire. We pick ourselves up. We choose a new and different path. We choose our own way. We choose to run our own race. We choose to persevere.

NOTES

1. *People Magazine*, 4 April 2017.
2. Viktor E. Frankl, *Man's Search for Meaning* (Boston, Mass.: Beacon Press, 2006).

CHAPTER 1

Grief and Mourning

If Jesus conquered sin and death, why do we grieve? Doesn't our faith protect us from grief, from pain and suffering? If our loved ones are in heaven or on their way there, are they not in the hands of God? And isn't this the goal of everyone, to get to heaven? So, if our loved ones are in heaven, shouldn't we be joyful?

It is true, that when our loved ones get to heaven they become saints. And as saints, they can intercede for us here on earth. We can have all the confidence in the world in the Paschal Mystery. We could have seen the empty tomb with our own eyes, but there still three problems. We are uncertain of their whereabouts, we miss them, and we are human. And so, we grieve our loss.

Faith does not protect us from suffering, and grief is suffering. Christ suffered an excruciating (Greek translation, crucified) death on a cross. He was not protected from suffering and neither are we. Christ died to redeem us, and to give us a path to heaven, but He did not die to save us from suffering in this life. Christ said, "Take up your cross… follow me." In other words, share in my suffering.

Jesus did not suffer alone. Simon helped carry His cross. His mother was with Him at Calvary when He took His last breath. And He does not want any of us to suffer alone either.

Our faith gives us hope, this confident expectation in an eternal life. But as humans, we have emotions. We have wants and desires, we have goals and plans. And though our loved ones might be in heaven, we are not. So, we grieve when someone we love dies because it leaves a void in our life, a big hole in our heart, and maybe some unanswered questions.

Grief Culture Years Ago

We live today in an antiseptic era where death is largely an unmentionable topic at the dinner table. But this has not always been the norm. During the agricultural era of the 1800s, 80% of the American population lived on rural farmlands. It was commonplace back then for family members, young and old, to see the death of a farm animal. Maybe the death was due to old age, or maybe due to the nature of running a for-profit farm. Or maybe for their own dinner that night.

The Victorian period in England of the mid to late 19th century is when the United States began the practice of mourning rituals. In 1861, Queen Victoria began the mourning customs by deciding to wear black after her husband, Prince Albert, died. She would wear black the rest of her life.

Between 1861 and 1865, the American Civil War took the lives of approximately 2% of the population, over 700,000. Many, not all bodies were recovered and returned home. America was grieving, and grieving Americans would begin the practice of mourning their dead. Some of the rituals included stopping the clocks to reflect the time of death and then starting them again after the deceased was buried. Widows would wear black for two years after her husband died. Mourning was largely a community event as people gathered around the deceased in solidarity for each other.

The first year after the death of her husband was called "deep mourning." During this time, she was to neither wear any jewelry nor accept any visitors. The next six months was called "half mourning." During this time, she could wear some white clothing. Then that last six months was called "light mourning" and she could wear other colors besides white and black. A widower would wear black as well, but often in the form of an arm band, and usually not as long. The length of mourning period differed, depending on whom the person was mourning. Mourning rituals were mainly practiced by those people "of means" who could afford the required attire and accessories.

In the late 1800s it was common for people to have picnics in cemeteries at their family lots. Graveyards then were the closest thing to modern-day public parks. So, people would gather with baskets of food and blankets and dine at the grave of their loved ones, undoubtedly engaging in conversations and sharing memories.

Mourning rituals began to fade after the turn of the century. With the beginning of World War I, grief became more of a pragmatic experience, with no time to mourn and no need for self-pity. Ten million died in this war. The United Kingdom had almost one million soldier and civilian deaths; the United States over 116,000. Due to the nature of the warfare, many bodies were never recovered, and with the sheer number of deaths, it made it impossible for many to be properly buried in a graveyard. The scale of this war had never been seen before. With bodies lost and often never returned, mourning rituals were also lost, and they have never returned to the scale that they once had.

Obstacles to Grieving Well

There are three obstacles to grieving well:

1. Our culture today,
2. We are ill-prepared,
3. We don't understand what grief is.

Our Culture Today

Today's culture wants us to grieve quickly, predictably and unemotionally. From a workshop that we held in 2015, a woman told us her story:

> Seven months after her husband of 59 years had died, the widow went to see her doctor for a physical—a sensible thing to do for any newly bereaved person. During the visit, she broke down and began crying. She expected to be consoled and comforted, instead, she was ridiculed. "If you are still crying six months after your husband's death, you must be depressed," the doctor told her.

This woman had spent over 700 months of her life with her husband. They raised children together, traveled together, balanced checkbooks together, and undoubtedly argued over trivial things—together. They had almost sixty Christmas celebrations! They went to countless funerals together. Over 700 months! And in a fraction of that time, her doctor finds it unacceptable for her to cry. That crying must be a sign of weakness or worse—depression. Couldn't she just feel sad? Couldn't she just miss someone badly enough to feel something? Depressives fear feelings. This woman wasn't fearing her feelings, she was expressing them in the form of tears. She wasn't depressed. She was grieving.

The latest version of the *Diagnostic and Statistical Manual for Mental Disorders* (DSM-5) carries over the two-week minimum duration period for bereavement. Essentially it says that if bereavement for an individual lasts more than two weeks, it could warrant a diagnosis, possibly depression, and then of course medication. To be sure, in some cases, bereavement could warrant a diagnosis of Major Depression, as the symptoms between the two are quite similar. But surely, two weeks is not enough time to make this evaluation. This is not to imply that all counselors will seek a quick diagnosis and reach to write a prescription. But it does speak to a collective cultural denial that loss is painful. That in most circumstances, two weeks is not nearly enough for someone to process this pain and begin to deal with the difficult emotions, let alone all the other issues that come attached to grief. The sooner we realize that grief is not a race to be won, but rather a loss to be acknowledged, accepted and absorbed into our life, the better we all will be. (We discuss this further in Chapter 6.)

Dr. Jean Twenge's book *iGen*,[1] is about today's super-connected kids and the problems they are facing in this super-connected world. Is it a coincidence that in 2012, people with iPhones passed the 50% threshold? And about this same time…

- More children began to feel sad, depressed and lonely,
- There was a 50% increase in clinical depression between 2011 and 2015,
- Dating and hanging out with friends dropped.

Twenge believes this is the worst mental health crisis in decades. In part because bullying doesn't stop at school, and it continues through social media. You must always look your best because you never know when an iPhone will take your picture. And parties you weren't invited to get publicly displayed on Facebook.

According to Occupational Therapist blogger Victoria Prooday:[2]

- One in five children have mental health issues,

- There is a 43% increase in ADHD,
- There is a 200% increase in suicide rates in children 10-14.

Prooday goes on to say that kids today are largely deprived of a healthy environment, which includes:

- Emotionally available parents (parents are also too digitally connected),
- Defined limits, responsibilities and guidance (too much entitlement),
- Balanced nutrition and adequate sleep,
- Exercise and social interaction,
- Downtime (no time to just be bored).

People over a certain age didn't grow up with a cellphone that has more technology than the first spacecraft that landed on the moon. Some of us know what a fax machine is and remember the ear-piercing sound slow speed internet made when connecting. But technology has pulled us all along and we have evolved to expect speed in everything. Name one thing that isn't completed faster today than it was ten years ago. Transportation? Communication? Manufacturing? Purchasing? Medicine? News? Service? Banking? If technology has had such an impact on an entire generation of millennials, how could it not have an impact on everyone else?

Technology is a blessing when used correctly and a curse when it is not. Automobiles have never been safer and never filled with more distractions. Our eyes are more off the road than on it. In 2016, 40,200 people died from automobile accidents, the most since 2007. Distracted driving is the number one killer of American teenagers. Texting while driving at 55mph equates to 100 yards, the length of a football field.

It is not just the millennials. We have become a generation of people who are connected to everything urgent, but seldom important.

Grief was once viewed with reverence and sympathy back in the nineteenth century, but now it seems as if it's a nuisance. It's as if there is a statute of limitations on our grief, with many of us trying to run out the clock. When we don't "recover" from it at the speed our culture has come to expect from everything else, we are viewed as sick. Grief interrupts. And who has time for that? We have things to do. Meetings to attend. Important deadlines to make. The kids need to be taken to soccer games and band practice. There is no time in our day to grieve. So, our world looks at a widow, who is still sad after six months, as pathological. Something must be wrong with her. She hasn't "snapped out" of her grief yet. She must be depressed. She must be medicated.

Grief has become a victim of our high-speed, high-tech world. How could it not? Grief however, as we have noted, is not a race to be won, but rather a loss to be mourned.

We Are Ill-Prepared

How well are we prepared for grief? How well are we equipped with the tools needed to navigate the often-lonely journey through a minefield of emotions? Are we fortified to withstand the after-shocks of loss, the tremors that reverberate up and down our spines for weeks, months or years after someone we love dies? How well do we prepare for the inevitable conclusion of someone's life and the changes that erupt like a volcano all around us, covering up everything that was who we were, forcing us to sprout new growth? For most of us, the answer is "not very well."

The facts are this. We spend most of our life in search of acquiring things, not losing them. From the time we leave the warmth of our mother's womb, we are in search of something. Oxygen. Without oxygen there is no need for anything else. But with it we continue our instinctual hunt for more. Nourishment. Warmth. Hygiene. Love. Touch. We cannot thrive without any of these essentials, in fact we will die if denied just one.

As we grow, our search for "more" expands to new and larger horizons. Our first bicycle. Toys. Clothes. Victories. Jewelry. Friendships. Relationships. Education. Marriage. Children. Job. A *better* job. A car. A *better* car. Travel. Fame. Fortune. A place to call home. A *better* place to call home. On and on it goes.

We grieve anything we love, are attached to and lose. It is our instinctive search for love that betrays us in the end. We are called to love. We are called to be in relationship with God, who is love. If we never open our hearts up to love, we will never feel the sudden sting of rejection and separation, but we may never feel *anything* at all.

What Grief Is

Let us define what grief is and then unpack it further. *Grief is a unique, mostly universal, automatic and multifaceted reaction to any loss, either real, anticipated or ambiguous.* The word grief comes the French word gréve, which means "a heavy burden." When it comes to the death of a loved one, grief is our reaction to a fragmented sense of self, we are something less than whole, an organic piece of us is missing. Because grief is a reaction, it is not meant to have a life-long identity or to be any measure of our self-worth. Our grief should ameliorate over time and slowly transform from a constant companion to an intermittent visitor, in which we pick the time and place to visit with our grief. In learning how to mourn, we come to accept our loss; we move it outside our body, always near us, but in a place where it can't harm us.

Grief is a Unique Reaction

For decades, we have been misinformed about grief. We have been led to believe that grief is predictable, that it follows a linear sequence of stages that we naturally move through on our way to healing. First, we deny or disbelieve, then we get angry, then we bargain with God, then we get depressed, and finally we accept. The stages of grief theory was originally posited by Elisabeth Kübler-Ross,[3] who was an early pioneer in the relatively new field of Thanatology, the study of death and dying. Dr. Kübler-Ross received 19 honorary degrees. She spent years studying patients who were dying and grieving their own impending death. Kübler-Ross devoted much of her life in helping hospice patients and even children to understand their grief.

The stage theory suggests that grief is passive, which it isn't. The old notion that time heals all wounds applies to the wounds of grief as well, but time alone is not the only factor in the healing process. The extent to which our wounds heal depends on the care, understanding and attentiveness we give them. Old wounds involving unresolved grief, usually stay unresolved unless we bring forth intention and action.

To suggest that grief follows a well-defined sequence minimizes the uniqueness of all our stories of who we are and who our loved ones were. Today, we no longer believe that grief happens in stages, rather that grief oscillates back and forth, up and down. There is no defined pattern to grief. There may be common emotions that many people share during their grief experience, yet it is still a unique experience for everyone who goes through it. Grief is ubiquitous yet is as unique as a fingerprint or a snowflake. Our lives are shaped by our unique DNA, our upbringing, our faith, our friends and our sex. And this is just the beginning of what makes grief unique.

In the Gospel account regarding the death of Lazarus (John 11), we see his sisters Martha and Mary have two very different initial reactions. Martha is quite angry at Jesus, contesting that if he had only come sooner Lazarus would not have died. Mary on the other hand, "sat in the house," perhaps being reflective and saddened by her loss. Only later did Mary come to Jesus, proclaiming the same thing, "Lord if you had been here, my brother would not have died." But Mary's reaction seems to be that of sadness. When Jesus saw her weeping, he was deeply moved in spirit, enough that he too was moved to tears.

J. William Worden and his *Four Tasks of Mourning*[4] has been credited with moving us away from the stage theory of grief, into that of mourning being a more active approach in which the griever takes responsibility for their healing. Worden also identified key factors that make our grief an individual experience:

- **Who the person was:** A spouse? A child? A parent? A close friend? A sibling? This is the most obvious, but we will grieve each loss differently, depending on the role this person played in our lives. It can be said that in losing a parent we lose part of our past. In losing a spouse we lose part of our present. In losing a child we lose part of our future. And in losing a sibling we lose part of our self.

- **The nature of the attachment:** John Bowlby[5] has formulated in his attachment theory that we are all born needing attachment to survive. As infants not only do we need someone to care for us by feeding, changing us and keeping us safe, but also we need to feel loved. This gives us a sense of security; as we grow, this attachment grows with us. Eventually our attachment expands to others as well. When death severs this attachment, powerful reactions occur, and we suffer from this loss.

- **How the person died:** Up until age 45, the two leading causes of death are accidents and suicide, each of which are sudden, and often violent and traumatic. These types of deaths cause an abrupt disruption and are grieved very differently than the death of someone who suffered from ALS or Alzheimer's. Was it an *ambiguous* loss where there is uncertainty about the death?

- **Emotional health of the griever:** Do we suffer from depression? Do we handle adversity and challenges well?

- **Coping styles and gender:** We all have our own coping styles when it comes to stress. What are they? Are we active or avoidant? Do we run into the flames of adversity and conflict, or run away from them? Men and women grieve differently too. Women tend to be more emotional and want to talk through their struggles, while men tend to want to get involved in some activity that will help them cope.

- **Social Support:** Often overlooked, yet how much support we have from friends and family plays a vital role in how we grieve. Do we have someone whom we can call when we need to talk? Or someone we can call in an emergency? Or someone who is just great fun to be around? We will discuss social support later as the Seventh Intention.

- **Cognitive Styles:** Are we ruminators? Do we let our minds run our lives? We will discuss this more later, when we discuss acceptance and the Third Intention.

For some, grief is paralyzing. What was once done with ease before grief, is now done with tremendous strain and effort. There may be what is called "mental inertia" where our brain just doesn't work as it once did. Under stress, our minds tend to focus on negative thoughts. "I'll never be well again!" I'll never be happy again!" And so on. What we think about affects how we feel, and how we feel affects what we think about.

Grief is Universal

People across all cultures grieve. Animals grieve. But even though it is a global phenomenon, it is still a distinct experience for everyone going through it.

Grief is Automatic

Grief is not one emotion, rather it comprises many emotions. Sadness, anger and guilt tend to be the more common emotions associated with grief. But there are many other emotions such as fear, anxiety, shame and loneliness to name just a few. C. S. Lewis said of his own grief after his wife died, "It's the price we pay for love." He said he never knew that grief felt so much like fear.

We grieve the loss of anything we love, feel attached to, or dependent on. A job, a friendship, our youth, our health, our financial security, and most certainly, a loved one who dies.

Sudden Loss

For many, loss comes suddenly—a car accident, a heart attack, or suicide. This type of death is very real and very abrupt and causes a sudden and dramatic disruption to their lives. These people grieve after the death of their loved one. They are thrown into a chaotic new world as they make funeral arrangements and phone calls, all while grieving.

Anticipated Loss

For others, grief begins after hearing a disturbing, perhaps terminal diagnosis. This might mean several months or several years that their loved one might have to live, but the process of grieving commences while their loved one is alive and continues after they have died. With anticipated loss, there is a sense of preparedness. There is often time for goodbyes from people who live far away. Funeral wishes can be discussed and planned for. Unlike with a sudden death, this process can be long and exhausting for months and years leading up to the death.

Ambiguous Loss

Ambiguous loss is an uncertain loss because a body was never recovered. A woman whom we know shared her story with us:

> The woman's son, while in Aruba, went out on a jet ski and was never seen again. This is like the Natalee Holloway story where the teenager vanished while vacationing in Aruba and was never seen again. Did the women's son drown and was his body eaten by sharks? Or was he kidnapped and is still alive? His mother along with the FBI searched for months. She held on to hope that he would be found again. Perhaps all these years later she still does. But the FBI eventually closed the case with no clear answer on

what happened.

The difficulty with ambiguous loss is deciding when to trade-in our last vestiges of hope, for what appears to be a conclusion with which we will need to come to terms. Only with the acceptance of death, can we begin to mourn.

Sudden Intruder

Grief is a sudden intruder. It knocks on our door when we least expect it. When we get a disturbing diagnosis about a loved one. Or when we get a phone call—there was an accident. Or when our loved one is simply with us one moment and gone the next.

Some prefer to close the door, pretend that none of this is happening. Disbelief doesn't change reality, it merely delays acting upon it. In the short-term, denial can be an effective coping mechanism, but at some point, the door must be opened. We must let grief in. We must deal with the pain that it causes.

> A young couple's child died soon after birth. Mom was a school teacher. Dad was a sculptor. Weeks later, and back to work, the woman came home, crawled upstairs and cried her eyes out on the bed. He was in his workshop in the basement, carving away at a tombstone for their child. Hearing her cries, he asked himself, "why can't I grieve like her?"

Some may think that they can "out-busy" their grief. That if I just keep busy enough I won't have to think about all my pain. Like denial, actively filling our lives with distractions so we don't face our emotions and struggles, is a short-term coping mechanism that could have long-term consequences. Grief is multifaceted—meaning, whatever affects us emotionally will affect us in so many other ways, including physically, cognitively, socially, spiritually and behaviorally. Grief can cause a rise in blood pressure, a weakened immune system, and an increase in blood sugar. Studies tell us our support system can dramatically change during the first year after a loss. We have a saying that strangers become friends, and friends become strangers.

There is a tendency to make grief a one-size-fits-all process. Grief is as unique as we are. We all have individual vulnerabilities. No two people were ever created the same. How we are raised is unique, because our parents are unique. Soon, doctors will be able to treat illness by developing treatments based upon each person's unique genetic structure. Medicines will then be prescribed to work with one's unique body chemistry.

This is crucial in understanding the mourning process—our paths on this journey will all be different. Grief is not a race, because there is no finish line. Grief is not static; it tends to ameliorate over time. Yet we mourn the rest of our lives. We adapt. We integrate. We heal. All at our own pace. We find our own way in different ways. We call this building our bridge to a new and different life.

Types of Grief

There are many types of grief. This book does not have the scope to list them all, but here are a few.

Healthy Grief

Please note that it is not called "normal grief." What is normal for some, might not be normal for others. For example, crying is a healthy expression of sadness, but for some, crying can be difficult, and might not be the way in which they express themselves.

It is estimated that about 90% of all grievers come to terms with their loss, express their emotions and process this loss in their own unique way. They are then able to move forward and resume living a healthy life. They find ways to mourn and have a continuing, albeit different, relationship with their loved one. They carry their cross the rest of their lives, but it becomes a weight that they can bear.

Disenfranchised Grief

Kenneth J. Doka, PhD,[6] Professor of Gerontology at the College of New Rochelle in New York, has written extensively about disenfranchised grief. The griever is disenfranchised when their loss is not recognized, supported or validated by their support system of family and friends. Often, insensitive comments, though not intentional, can trigger feelings of hurt and anger. Without even knowing it, the griever is disenfranchised, and these comments can make the person feel as though they are doing something wrong, which can suppress or delay the mourning process.

When Jesus needed his disciples the most, where were they? They all scattered. He predicted that they would, and they did. This is what happens when someone is disenfranchised in their grief. Their support system isn't there for them in a validating, comforting way. Instead, they criticize, deflect, minimize or don't acknowledge at all.

Three Primary Ways That Disenfranchised Grief Occurs

1) The relationship is not socially recognized or is minimized: The level of attachment determines the level of grief. When the relationship is not socially recognized, the level of support given the griever does not seem commensurate with the pain that the griever feels from this loss. An example is an ex-spouse. Perhaps the divorce took place many years before; family and friends have since moved on, yet the griever may still retain some bond of attachment. Perhaps they had children together. There is still a sense of loss worth mourning.

> At our first workshop, a woman shared that her husband had died from alcoholism. Her family didn't understand her pain. He just should have stopped drinking. She was made to feel guilty for not doing more. When discussing disenfranchised grief, the woman stood up and proudly proclaimed, "finally someone understands what I'm going through!"

A pregnancy loss is considered the "loneliest grief" of all. Although prospective grandparents and aunts and uncles will surely grieve this loss too, the impact on the mother and father is quite different and more profound. One in ten pregnancies will end in a miscarriage during the first twenty weeks, or a stillbirth after twenty weeks. There is a tendency in some cases to try to minimize this loss, as if that will take away the pain. Comments such as, "you can have more children," or "be thankful you have other children," disenfranchise the grieving parents, because they are made to feel that this child does not warrant the pain they feel.

The loss of a grandparent at ninety-five years old can also get minimized—"They lived a long life. Why are you sad?"

Any relationship in which the deceased is not recognized or otherwise minimized, and the griever's grief is not supported or validated, provides an opportunity for disenfranchised grief.

2) The way the person died is socially unspeakable: Suicide is the one type of death where two questions are asked; *Why did they do it?*

Why didn't I prevent them from doing it? Suicide transfers the pain from the one who took their life, to those left to grieve.

Homicide, abortion, alcoholism and drug overdoses are other common deaths that carry a social stigma that sometimes results in shame for the griever. Again, when the griever doesn't feel supported and otherwise feels under attack from his/her social network, they will often feel disenfranchised.

3) The Griever is not grieving as expected: Here, the griever is not grieving as their social network believes and accepts as "normal." Perhaps they are too emotional, or not emotional enough. Or they are grieving too long.

Complicated Grief

Complicated Grief, or Persistent Complex Bereavement Disorder, is a type of grief in which the griever seems "stuck" in a persistent state of acute grief. Something is blocking them from accepting and adapting to their loss. Complicated Grief could be due to the nature of the loss, e.g., suicide; to the nature of the bond, or to the emotional state of the griever before the loss. Complicated grief, found in about 7% to 10% of all grieving people, requires professional intervention. We elaborate upon it under the topic of depression.

Mourning

If grief is our reaction to loss, then mourning is our *intentional response*. It is how we express our grief. It is what we do with the pain that we feel after someone whom we love dies. Mourning is our call to piece together again an imperfect tapestry into our imperfect world and restore an imperfect good. Mourning is a life-long mission of reaching back on what was, reaching forward on what can be, and simply finding our way to a new world.

Mourning is largely a learned behavior. It helps us to gain back some sense of control because we are taking charge of the situation in which we find ourselves. With mourning, we find healthy ways to express our thoughts and feelings.

We might want to look at grief as lent, the forty days in our own desert, sometimes alone, wandering aimlessly, longing to be with the one we lost. Can it be said that our grief journey culminates when we pick up our own cross? When we surrender like Jesus did? When we suffer like Jesus did? When we forgive like Jesus did?

Might we be wise to then consider mourning as our Easter Sunday?… a time of great hope… a time of rebirth and renewal… a time of grace… a time of solidarity… a time of transformation.

The next few topics are some brief examples of mourning; more details will be given with each of the Seven Intentions of Mourning.

Praying

We'll discuss prayer in more in depth in the First Intention, but spending time with our Lord, even ten minutes a day will help to quiet our minds and focus our attention on and with the great healer.

Crying

Jesus is our role model on how to grieve. How many times in the gospels do we see him showing human emotions, such as compassion and sorrow? When his friend Lazarus died, he wept. Tears release toxins from our bodies. They are healthy and even curative, for both men and women.

Journaling

Putting our feelings into words, either written or verbal is powerful and healing. This helps us to express our deepest thoughts and emotions in a safe place.

Exercising

Exercise is a great stress reliever because it raises a body's positive hormones. Even a ten- to fifteen-minute brisk walk is helpful. Exercise has been shown to help treat depression, because it changes the chemistry of one's brain in a manner similar to anti-depressant drugs. Of course, speak with your doctor before beginning an exercise program.

Talking

People who can identify their feelings and find the words to express them are the quickest to gain back some control. "People who can make a coherent story about what happened cope much better with the death than people who don't."[7]

Laughing

Crying has always been associated with grief, but now we know that laughing is just as important. Laughter gives us moments of rest—often a much-needed time-out—from the burden we carry. Studies have shown that when grievers can share stories about their loved ones and express genuine laughter, it is predictive of a better adjustment to the loss.

Collective Mourning

Social media platforms, such as Facebook and Twitter, have become popular tools for grievers to go online and post or tweet their thoughts, feelings and sentiments for someone who died, in an internet community environment. In many ways, this is the modern version of how we mourned in the nineteenth century, where the plows would stop, and the community gathered together to collectively console one another. Another example is a roadside memorial, where mourners place flowers and pictures at the place where an accident occurred to remember a deceased loved one.

NOTES

1. Jean M. Twenge, "Have Smartphones Destroyed a Generation?" *The Atlantic*, September 2017.
2. Victoria Prooday, "The Silent Tragedy Affecting Today's Children," *YourOT. com*, May 2017.
3. Elisabeth Kübler-Ross, M.D., *On Death and Dying*. (NYC: Macmillan, 1969).
4. J. William Worden, *Grief Counseling and Grief Therapy*, 4th Ed. New York: Springer Publishing Company, 2009.
5. John Bowlby, Wikipedia. https://en.wikipedia.org/wiki/John_Bowlby.
6. Kenneth J. Doka, *Disenfranchised Grief, Recognizing Hidden Sorrow*. New York: Springer Publishing Company, 1989.
7. Illene Cupit, Professor of Human Development, University of Wisconsin.

 JOHANN WOLFGANG VON GOETHE

How can we learn to know ourselves? Never by reflection but action. Try to do your duty and you will soon find out what you are. But what is your duty? The demands of the day.

CHAPTER 2

Mourning With Intention

Viktor Frankl, in his inspiring book, *Man's Search for Meaning*,[1] wrote, "we find meaning in our suffering by the ways we choose to respond to it." Frankl asserted that we find meaning in life by what we achieve in life, how we experience life and our attitude toward life. That in choosing our response to whatever happens, we take responsibility for our actions. It is in these decisions that we make and the actions in which we carry them out that we find meaning and fulfillment.

> Frankl once had a conversation with an elderly man who was depressed over the death of his wife. Frankl asked him, "What would have happened if you had died first and your wife would have survived you?"
>
> "Oh," the man replied, "for her this would have been terrible; how she would have suffered." "You see," said Frankl, "such a suffering has been spared her; and it is you who have spared her this suffering; but now, you have to pay for it by surviving her and mourning her."
>
> The man did not say a word. He shook Frankl's hand and calmly walked out of his office.

Mourning is our intentional response to grief. This is the good news. There are tangible, practical, actionable things we can do that will help us heal our wounds from loss and have an enduring connection with our loved ones.

To have intention is to be *conscious* of what we want to experience or create. This is important because we spend far too much of our lives unaware of the present moment. We are usually searching in our minds backwards to what we did ten minutes ago or ten years ago, or forwards to what we want to do ten minutes or ten years in the future. With intention, we make reasonable plans, but we pay full attention to what is happening now.

When we mourn with intention we are actively involved. Not in fixing our pain. But in accepting it and in changing it. To a large extent, our culture today wants to ignore grief. It wants us to move on without ever facing reality. When we mourn with intentionality, we face our fears and our struggles. We are conscious about our grief and conscious of how we want to experience this journey. And it *is* a journey. It is a process. It doesn't so much end as it changes.

Intentional mourning is a process of making good choices that help us to experience the fullness and the "isness" of who this person was, or people were, who died. Yet we also begin to understand who *we* are post-loss and who we will be going forward. In making these choices on how we mourn, we begin to gain back some sense of control in an otherwise uncontrollable universe, which spins on an axis foreign to us.

When we are grieving, the world we live in is often unfamiliar. Nothing seems as it was anymore. The routine of life we enjoyed and maybe took for granted vanishes in an instant. This is true whether our loss is sudden and unexpected, or anticipated for some time. And it will never be as it once was. Never. This might be the first thing we need to accept. There is no going back to our pre-loss lives. They are gone forever.

But though yesterday is lost, in tomorrow there is hope. "Through many tribulations we must enter the Kingdom of God" (Acts 14:22). Losing a loved one forces us to make many choices. Yet the most important choice of all is how we respond to this loss. Do we accept this loss as a permanent defeat, or a major change in our lives? Do we accept the fact that this loss will take time to process and work through? That our lives are forever changed, but in trials can come learning and growth. In pain can come new meaning and mission. When our suffering is aligned with the cross, we become servants, helping others heal, as we heal ourselves. We become disciples of hope.

Love is not practiced in a vacuum. We must *express* love to *feel* love. Newborn babies would fail to thrive if they didn't feel love from another. All relationships require active participation and, yes, work. Intention is like love, it's a verb. It requires thinking and action.

Our oldest son, Eric O'Shaughnessy, spent 110 days hiking the Appalachian Trail—2,168 miles, Georgia to Maine, about 20 miles per day. When asked how he did this he simply replied, "I put one foot in front of the other and walked. But with each step I thought about the end of the trail and how I was going to feel when I got to the top of Mount Katahdin (in Maine)." He knew where he was going, and he mostly knew how to get there. He didn't know all the pitfalls that he would face along the way, but he knew that he would keep pushing forward. He had a vision. He was very intentional each day. He was conscious of what he wanted to do and how he wanted to achieve his goal.

In the movie, "Touching the Void,"[2] two climbers made it to the summit of the west face of the Siula Grande Mountain in the Peruvian Andes Mountains, over 20,000 feet above sea level. Their climb had never been attempted before. On the way down, one of climbers fell and broke his tibia. The two were tied together with a rope, but during the decent, the healthy climber was forced to cut the rope to save his own life. The wounded climber was thought to be dead, but over the course of three days, in small, incremental crawls, in freezing temperatures, he negotiated his way down the mountain and survived. His intention was to survive and the only way to survive was to work his way down the mountain.

We don't need to hike the Appalachian Trail or climb to the top of a mountain. Yet when we are intentional, we are conscious of what we want to create. Little things are intentional, yet they can lead to big results. The wounded climber set goals to crawl twenty feet. And then another twenty feet. These series of goals led him down the mountain and to safety.

The Seven Intentions of Mourning

The Seven Intentions of Mourning are conscious choices. They are not steps, stages, or tasks. They are not a one-size-fits-all model. Each intention has its own unique purpose in helping to heal the wounds of the unique person who is using them—you! The Seven Intentions have the acronym of PRAYERS.

1. Prayer

2. Remember and Honor

3. Acceptance

4. Yield to the Pain of our Suffering

5. Enduring Connection

6. Rebuild, Redefine, Reinvent

7. Support—Give and Receive

Two Paths

When we mourn with intention, we begin to follow two paths. There is an inward path that tends to be reflective and emotional, where we humbly glance back at *what was* while trying to come to terms with *what is*. Then there is an outward path that tends to be collaborative and engaging. It is on this path that we begin to look forward, as disciples of hope, towards a future of *what can be*. On this path we begin to see that our suffering, if we are open to God's grace, can be redemptive and meaningful, where a bridge to a new and different life is often revealed.

Neither path is better than the other. They both have their own painful challenges. Each must be walked.

These are the Intentions for the *inward* path:

1. **Prayer** is found on both the inward and outward path. Prayer is the "soul" of the Christian life. It is our search for the invisible God, through an encounter with His risen Son. It is a reaching inward and outward, "But when you pray, go into your room and shut the door and pray to your Father who is in secret; and your Father who sees in secret will reward you" (Matt 6:6).

2. **Remember and Honor** our loved ones means treasuring the gifts that they left us: the memories, the linking objects and how they helped to shape our lives. Simple rituals are meaningful expressions of love that help us transition from one life to another.

3. **Acceptance** is coming to terms with what has happened. It is felt in our hearts and interpreted by our minds. Acceptance does not alleviate our suffering, but it does allow us to begin the journey to create meaning and purpose in our suffering.

4. **Yield to the pain** means that we acknowledge and face our moral and physical suffering to fully grieve our loss. We swim *with* the current, our present situation, and not *against* it.

These are the Intentions for the *outward* path:

5. An **enduring connection** extends the bonds forged in life that have been cut short by death, and attempts to reconstruct the relationship in a personal and meaningful way. It is different than an event or ceremony, which looks inward; it is a mission of redemptive healing that looks outward.

6. **Redefining and rebuilding** our lives looks outward, at life apart from our loved one. What are our new roles and priorities? What are our new hopes, dreams and plans? What is our new relationship with the world?

7. Grief is best when it is **socially supported**, and publicly mourned. In seeking to help others, we become disciples of hope. In receiving help from others, we recognize the Body of Christ.

When it comes to **The Seven Intentions of Mourning**, we will see how Jesus is our role model. He **prayed** constantly, often alone on a mountain. The rituals that we practice at every Mass, is done so to **remember** His death, His resurrection, and His sacrifice for all of us. He **accepted** His ministry with great love and great courage, even unto death. He wept, He **yielded to the pain** that He felt in that moment. Through our prayer and the Eucharist, we have an **enduring connection** with Him; likewise through His promise, we have an **enduring connection** with our loved ones in heaven. When God became man, He **redefined** our relationship with Him through Christ. He asks all of us to participate in His Church, as one body in Christ and **support** each other. When one of us suffers, we all suffer.

The Catholic Funeral Liturgy

The Seven Intentions are also seen in one form or another in the days before, during and after the funeral liturgy. The funeral liturgy is very intentional, filled with rituals, and with our one main goal—to pray our loved one home.

From the moment of death, The Church enters one continuous **prayer**. *"At the death of a Christian, the Church intercedes on behalf of* *the deceased because of its confident belief that death is not the end, nor does in break the bonds forged in life."* Praying for the dead is holy and pious with powers to free them from their sins.[3]

In the time leading up to the funeral, stories about the deceased are told, pictures are displayed, and videos shown. We **remember** the times we had together, as well as **honor** and celebrate a life that was lived.

There may be no greater way to **accept** the death of a loved one, than an open casket and their lifeless body in it. Their soul is in transition, so we gather to pray them into the hands of God. Yet the funeral liturgy is also for the bereaved, the church militant. The funeral helps us to begin the painful process of acknowledging their death and accepting it in our hearts and minds.

Other than weddings, perhaps the most emotional event in our life is a funeral. Here we have full permission to weep as Jesus did and to **yield to our pain**. But though tears are often seen at funerals, it is common to witness laughter as well. Our emotions, whatever they are, should never be ignored, they are meant to be felt and expressed.

As previously mentioned, death does not break the bonds forged in life. This **enduring connection** is sustained through prayer as well as other ways which may come long after the funeral. While this intention of having a continuing bond with our loved one is witnessed initially through prayer, it can also be processed in other ways, which we'll discuss more, that extend into a mission that helps good come from bad.

At funerals we are faced with the thought of our own mortality. The **rebuild** intention is about how we adapt to the loss. This process can take months or years, but the role of who we now are can begin much sooner. If we have lost both our parents, we are now orphaned. If we have lost our spouse, we are widowed. If we have children and have lost our spouse, we are an only-parent.

The funeral is often the time when we feel the most **support**, a sense of community and fellowship, and where friends and family come to express their condolences. Grief must be **socially supported** to be publicly mourned. If there is ever a public place to mourn, it's at a funeral.

When we mourn with intention we are actively involved in our healing. We pray. We have confidence that our loved ones are in the circle, the great cloud of witnesses, cheering us on. When we acknowledge our suffering, and mount it to the cross of Christ, it has meaning and purpose. Somehow, we become an instrument of God's love and power where through Him anything is possible; where through Him, good can pour forth from bad.

NOTES

1. Viktor E. Frankl, *Man's Search for Meaning*, Boston, Mass.: Beacon Press, 2006.
2. *Touching the Void*. Film. U.K.: FilmFour Productions, 2003.
3. *Order of Christian Funerals*.

 JACQUES PHILLIPE

Whatever our trials and disappointments, prayer makes us rediscover enough strength and hope to take up our lives again with total confidence in the future.

CHAPTER 3

The First Intention: Prayer

PRAYERFUL

But when you pray, go to your inner room, close the door, and pray to your Father in secret. And your Father who sees in secret will repay you. (MATT 6:6)

Let us pray. *In the name of the Father, and of the Son and the Holy Spirit.*

Memorare: Remember, O most gracious Virgin Mary, that never was it known that anyone who fled to thy protection, implored thy help, or sought thine intercession was left unaided. Inspired by this confidence, I fly unto thee, O Virgin of virgins, my mother; to thee do I come, before thee I stand, sinful and sorrowful. O Mother of the Word Incarnate, despise not my petitions, but in thy mercy hear and answer me. Amen.

Elizabeth Ann Seton, pray for us.

The Parable of the Widow and the Unrighteous Judge

And he told them a parable, the effect that they ought always to pray and not lose heart. He said, "In a certain city, there was a judge who neither feared God nor regarded man; and there was a widow in that city who kept coming to him and saying, 'Vindicate me against my adversary.' For a while he refused, but afterwards he said to himself, 'Though I neither fear God nor regard man, yet because this widow bothers me, I will vindicate her, or she will wear me out by her continual coming.'" And the Lord said, "Hear what the unrighteous judge says. And will not God vindicate his elect, who cry to him day and night? Will he delay long over them? I tell you, he will vindicate them speedily. Nevertheless, when the son on man comes, he will find faith on earth." (LUKE 18:1-8)

PRACTICAL

This chapter began in two places. One, sitting alongside the shores of Lake Michigan listening to the soothing melody of the waves while the soul-soothing breezes washed away worry. The other, in Adoration; no better place for an unencumbered connection with our Lord. Matthew 6:6 directs us to pray by first going to our inner room. This harkens back to the Holy of Holies, which was the innermost sacred room where God dwelled in the ancient tabernacle of Moses in Jerusalem. Only the high priest could enter—and only once a year, on Yom Kippur, the Day of Atonement. Here is one key for our entry into prayer; finding our inner room. And that inner room can become even more difficult to find when our hearts are grieving the death of someone, or a few someones, whom we so dearly loved and lost. Life is so unfair and cruel. As we ask the answer-less why's, praying helps us to find out *how*. How to live again after loss.

There is no order to the Seven Intentions of Mourning except with the intention of Prayer. If we do not begin all that we do in prayer, it will not bear fruit. Prayer is the seed we plant from which God's guidance is harnessed and can grow what may seem out of reach into the possible. Prayer is our foundation.

What is Prayer?

What prayer is and means to you is personal; it's a matter of your heart. Vital is to root it, however, in Christ and a mixture of Catholic guidance. St. Thérèse of Lisieux defines prayer, "For me, prayer is a surge of the heart; it is a simple look turned toward heaven, it is a cry of recognition and of love, embracing both trial and joy."[1] In *Thirsting for Prayer,* Jacques Philippe writes, "The first thing that should motivate us and encourage us to enter into a life of prayer is that God himself is inviting us to do it. Man searches for God, but God seeks out man even more actively... in prayer there is a mystery that absolutely surpasses our understanding."[2]

> **PRAYER**
>
> Prayer is both an inward- and outward-looking intention. It is taking time each day to be in communion with God. To be still. And in the silence, listen. Then respond to what you hear.

For me, prayer is the space and time that we go to in our hearts when there is nowhere else to go with our pain, worries, questions, suffering, or the anguish of the emptiness of loss. A priest friend once reminded me of a quote by Corrie Ten Boom, author of *The Hiding Place* and a Dutch watchmaker and Christian who, along with her father and other family members, helped many Jews escape the Nazi Holocaust during World War II by hiding them in her closet; "There is no pit so deep, that God's love is not deeper still."[3]

Praying can be elusive in the middle of loss and our "go" culture. You sit down, kneel, find a space... and then nothing. No words come to mind. You know prayer would be the perfect thing to do, yet nothing but air. What can you say or ask of a Lord when your loved one, or loved ones, should be with you? The landscape of prayer can feel like a mirage in a desert; elusive and out of reach. We aren't good at becoming human beings—we are "human doings." Over two million emails are sent every second. We send six billion text messages every day in the U.S. According to a report released by Sanford C. Bernstein, Amazon ships an average of 608 million packages each year.[4]

No wonder we can't, don't want to, or struggle with prayer. Do we ever stop? Until death knocks us off our feet and we lose our bearings. Oddly enough, this poises us well to enter prayer. The *Catechism of the Catholic Church* says, "Prayer is the raising of one's mind and heart to God or the requesting of good things from God. But when we pray, do we speak from the height of our pride and will, or out of the depths of a humble and contrite heart? He who humbles himself will be exalted; humility is the foundation of prayer; only when we humbly acknowledge that 'we do not know how to pray as we ought,' are we ready to receive freely the gift of prayer. 'Man is a beggar before God'" (CCC §2559).

Oh, how in grief our hearts have been humbled. We know in a profound and intimate way there is so little over which we have control. We understand that life can be ripped from us as quickly as a tide, or over a long excruciating battle. Humbled we are. "Be still and know that I am God!" (Ps 46:11). This is where prayer begins—in humble stillness.

Why Pray?

The last thing we may think we have time for, is the first thing we should be doing. Simply, prayer helps us and our loved ones too; it's all about connecting.

How Prayer Helps Us

When we are mourning, there are, out of many, two fruits of prayer that are powerful for us to keep in mind. One fruit is peace—we slow down, if only for a moment, and thus we slow the world down with us. And peace ushers in healing. After my first husband David died the void his absence left behind was without end; like trying to see the other side of Lake Michigan from the shoreline. Cars kept moving, people kept working, the hands of the clock never stopped. I so badly wanted time and the world to stop, for a second or two, to acknowledge that David was gone. I yelled one time, "Just stop!" The world wouldn't listen, but God did, in prayer. It was amid slowly praying the rosary that time finally halted. The roll of every bead became an intentional pause—each bead a touchpoint of peace. The rosary may not be your way and that's okay. Perhaps it's *Lectio Divina* or praying with scripture to bring into the present moment the message that God has for us today, now. I remember one time during my own mourning journey, entering into prayer with scripture, deciding to read—aloud—in the *Acts of the Apostles* about Paul's travels to spread the salvific message of Christ. Unexpectedly, I was moved to tears. An example of the power of the Living Word of God; the hardships of Paul's travels reminded me my own "shipwrecked life." He kept going, and so could I. Maybe Adoration is your place for prayer or journaling. Finding or enhancing your prayer life is key in grief because it brings us calm amidst our storms, opens us up to cry good tears, and slows the spinning earth just enough to carve out a healing place in our hearts. God knows exactly where that place is. Better than anyone else.

The second fruit of prayer is grace, which is power. In prayer we tap into the mightiness of a relationship with Jesus. Fleming Rutledge wrote in *The Crucifixion* that "Jesus proclaimed as Lord in the New Testament comes closer than any other figure known to human history to being universal, transcending time and historical location, belonging to all cultures and all people everywhere and forever."[5] To drill home this point, and the why and power of prayer, Luke Timothy Johnson, in his book *The Real Jesus: The Misguided Quest of the Historical Jesus and the Truth of the Traditional Gospels* wrote, "Christian faith is based on religious claims concerning the present power of Jesus…"[6] The power of our prayer taps into the power of Christ and it's that power we must call upon, in a particular way, when we are mourning. We must pray our way into Jesus so that the tears we cry are blended into His.

How Prayer Helps Our Loved Ones

Often in our ministry we've been asked how we know where our loved ones are. Did they go straight to heaven? Are they in purgatory? Hell? Many question and worry because they know of lives not lived perfectly, faithfully, and there's "undone" stuff lingering. Have some comfort in knowing that God predestines no one to go to hell (CCC §1037). In other words, He wants us all with Him. At the moment of death, there is an immediate and particular judgement (CCC §1022). When we die, our "résumé" is before God and shows all the details of how we lived our lives. What was done, is done. What was said, is said. There is no do-over. In death we can no longer pray for ourselves. But there is hope and we can't even come close to knowing either the mind of God or His infinite mercy at the instant that our loved ones died.

We can also find some help here: "From the beginning the Church has honored the memory of the dead and offered prayers in suffrage for them, above all the Eucharistic sacrifice, so that, thus purified, they may attain the beatific vision of God" (CCC §1032). There is power in our prayers for our loved ones! In prayer the love of God and our loved ones are nourished, tapped into, and strengthened. Death doesn't have the final say; through prayer we can remain in relationship with those we can no longer embrace. Through prayer we get to pray our loved ones, and others, home—to heaven—because they cannot. This is significant motivation to pray for us, the Church Militant, here on earth and is a great example of redemptive mourning, which we pose in greater detail in the Fifth Intention. As we mourn, we can play a role in saving souls and eventually being united with our cherished family and friends in sharing the beatific vision.

Connection

Hebrews 12:1 reminds us, "We are surrounded by so great a cloud of witnesses..." These witnesses are the angels and saints in heaven who intercede for us from their heavenly home and cheer us on. They are our eternal faith coaches who are a part of the mystical body of Christ. It is vital that we tap into this bounty of support that stretches from heaven into our hearts. We should ask for their intercession daily.

Saint Thérèse of Lisieux said that she would spend her eternity doing good on earth. Saint Dominic, on his deathbed, said to his brothers at his side that he did not want them to weep for him because he knew that he would be more useful to them after his death and would then be more effective in his help to them (CCC §956).

Our saints in heaven are busy and are cheering us on, especially so, I believe, when we are troubled. One of David's favorite songs was Simon and Garfunkel's "Bridge Over Troubled Water."[7] The lyrics speak to feeling weary and small, often teary-eyed, and friendless. That bridge from sadness to acceptance is more easily crossed when someone is on your side. In times when sadness brings us down, our Saints are ready to lay themselves down in order to prop us up. These words bring home the point and instill an image that we should call upon when grief beckons: our Saints laying themselves down to prop us up when sadness brings us down.

Suggestions for Prayer

Before Your Feet Hit the Floor

Don't let your feet hit the floor, or begin your morning, without acknowledging our Lord and asking for His help in living the day given to you. Admittedly, the day may feel, upon waking, like a dreary heavy blanket that you want to hide under and make this nightmare of loss disappear. But, Christ awaits us and invites us to arise with Him in mind.

Our pastor shared a story with us about two shepherds. One awoke in the early morning to take his flock into fields covered with the morning dew. The sheep ate and were hydrated and for the rest of the day they rested. The other shepherd slept late, and when he took his flock into the fields, their day was spent scrambling here and there to find food and water. Let us begin each day giving God the first fruits of our morning—and our mourning. To mourn with intention means to start each day, before your feet hit the floor, with prayer.

Keep It Simple

St. Thérèse of Lisieux, our saint of the little ways of faith, offered small sacrifices for love. Whether it was a smile, or a kind word, she did the smallest of things with great love. Saint Teresa of Calcutta lived her life doing simple things with great love.

Keep it simple. Grief has very long tentacles. It makes its way into every nook and cranny of our lives and brains. Knowing that prayer in the midst of grief can be absent or minimal, for many of us, simplicity is helpful. A great thing to say each morning is, "Lord, thank You for this day. May Your light shine through me in it." Even "Help me, Lord!" goes straight to the ears of God.

And there are certainly times when we don't even have the words. It is here that we tell God just that "God, I don't have the words, please help me find them." There is a saying that some people come into our lives for a reason, season, or a lifetime. Maybe it's a co-worker, a family member, or a friend-of-a-friend who has crossed paths with you in this season of loss when your prayer life has run out of steam. If you can't find the words, or even if you can, ask them for help. Ask them to be your prayer warrior, to pray for you when you can't. It's a simple ask that we often do not think to make.

Write It Down

We spent a year writing our journal "Finding the Words," with those who grieve in mind. When we are at a loss for what to say, sometimes writing helps. You don't need to be a "writer" to write. In taking pen or pencil to paper nothing must be spelled correctly, sound nice, or even make sense. You can be completely vulnerable and honest when the rest of the world wants you to "snap out of it." Writing, or journaling, is a form of prayer and all it must be is a sentence or a word.

For the years in which David battled while my mom was paralyzed and in a fight for her life, no verbal expression could come close to describing the pain and trauma of it all. So, writing made sense. Ink was a processing agent. The paper seemed to soak up what my heart could not. It was a coping mechanism; it was healing, and a tool for prayer. Some pages contain one-word entries, others several paragraphs. No rules. And how nice that was when grief can "rule over" us. It all began with a ninety-nine-cent composition notebook from the local grocery store. Consider this God's nudge; it may be the best ninety-nine cents you spend in a while.

Talk It Out

Our pastor has said this a few times, "Most of the people I talk to are dead." A bit crass perhaps but we should be asking for the help of those who have gone before us—we've been doing it for years! From the year A.D. 400, St. Augustine's words are current and relevant now, "A Christian people celebrates together in religious solemnity the memorials of the martyrs, both to encourage their being imitated and so that it can share in their merits and be aided by their prayers."[8] Love never ends.

It's okay to seek their aid, to ask them where they are, to ask for their guidance and intercession, and to tell them that we love them and miss them. It isn't crazy; it is an aspect of living and healing within our faith.

Years ago, after David had been gone a few months, I heard something rattling in our kitchen. For a fleeting split second, it felt as if he were in the room just over my right shoulder. So, I said, "David, if you're going to be clanking around in there, would you mind making some dinner too?!" Laughter mixed with healing tears. Having a conversation with an invisible person in front of the check-out clerk at the grocery store is one thing; but during a run or a walk or for a time in our private "inner room" is healthy.

Create Your Inner Room

"Is prayer your steering wheel, or your spare tire?" A friend of mine has a certain chair in her home that she calls her "prayer chair." It's where she sits and prays, and the family knows that's her special spot to seek and listen to God.

Creating a devoted place for prayer in your home welcomes the movement of the Spirit, of God, of Christ into the void of loss so they can accompany you. There, you are not alone. Keeping it simple works here too. Pick your ingredients: a comfortable place to sit, a Bible, a candle, a rosary. When you define your space, you'll be more likely to visit it. Praying will have a priority because you've given it a home within your home. Your "inner room" leads to well-being.

Summary

The Seven Intentions of Mourning are in no certain order except prayer. We should begin our day, our decisions, our lives in prayer. It is one of the most powerful healing tools we have to help us mourn. Saint Padre Pio, known for his piety and charity, said this: "Prayer is the best weapon we have; it is the key to God's heart. You must speak to Jesus not only with your lips, but [also] with your heart. In fact, on certain occasions you should only speak to Him with your heart."[9]

We who are grieving are in a unique yet painful circumstance to enter into prayer with a rightful disposition, because we have been offered the grace and virtue of humility. Literally or figuratively, we've been brought to our knees in the anguish of loss.

There is so much we may not have the energy to do. Grief is exhausting. Yet, amid feeling powerless or tapped out, our prayer cannot only help our own souls but the souls of others; both here on earth and heaven bound. Keeping it simple and inviting someone to be your prayer warrior can be invaluable. Speak to God. Speak to your loved one. Find your "inner room" and go there often. There, you will always meet Christ who awaits to listen, speak, and be in relationship with you, in a special way, on the pathway of grief and mourning.

PERSONAL

Questions to reflect on:

If you could ask God any question, what would it be?

In creating your "inner room," what are the most important and meaningful elements for you to have?

What are the obstacles in your prayer life that you could work on removing?

Works of Mercy: Praying for the Living and the Dead

Consider spending one hour each week in Eucharistic Adoration praying for someone living and one deceased. Request a Mass intention for a family member or friend.

Take some quiet time to write...

Your First Intention: Prayer

It is my intention to...

Example: *It is my intention to make time every morning to read scripture and pray.*

NOTES

1. St. Thérèse of Lisieux, *Manuscrits autobiographiques*, C 25r., in *CCC §2558*.
2. Jacques Philippe, *Thirsting for Prayer*. New Rochelle, NY: Scepter Publishers, Inc., 2014, p. 7.
3. Corrie Ten Boom, *The Hiding Place*, 1974.
4. Sanford C. Bernstein cited in "How Many Cardboard Boxes Does Amazon Ship Each Day?", *MrBoxOnline*. 15 September 2016. https://blog.mrboxonline.com/corrugated/how-many-cardboard-boxes-does-amazon-ship-each-day/, accessed 27 July 2018.
5. Fleming Rutledge, *The Crucifixion*. William B. Eerdmans Publishing Company, 2015, p. 29.
6. Luke Timothy Johnson, *The Real Jesus: The Misguided Quest of the Historical Jesus and the Truth of the Traditional Gospels*. New York Harper Collins, 1996, p. 133-43
7. Simon & Garfunkel, *Bridge Over Troubled Water*. Columbia Records, 26 January 1970.
8. St. Augustine, "Against Faustus the Manichean," *Contra Faustum*, Book XXII.
9. St. Padre Pio, *Words of Light*. Paraclete Press, 2000.

 PHYLLIS SILVERMAN

Death robs us of a present and a future with our loved ones, but it has no grip on the past. Memories are the most precious gifts survivors are left with.

CHAPTER 4

The Second Intention: Remember and Honor

PRAYERFUL

This is my body which is for you. Do this in remembrance of me. (1 Cor 11:24)

Let us pray. *In the name of the Father, and of the Son and the Holy Spirit.*

Father, we give thanks for our many blessings and gifts, especially the gift of your Son who has conquered death and restored life. But today, I feel like one of your lost sheep. Find me. Help me to mourn with great hope. Help me to heal my wounds of loss. Help me to navigate my path to a new and different life. Help me to come to know You in a profound way. I ask this all in your Son's name. Amen

Elizabeth Ann Seton, pray for us.

The Parable of the Lost Sheep

Now the tax collectors and sinners were all drawing near to him. And the Pharisees and the scribes murmured, saying, "This man receives sinners and eats with them."

So, he told them a parable: What man of you, having

a hundred sheep, if he has lost one of them, does not leave the ninety-nine in the wilderness, and go after the one which is lost, until he finds it? And when he finds it, he lays it on his shoulders and rejoices. And when he comes home, he calls together his friends and his neighbors, saying to them, 'Rejoice with me, for I have found my sheep which was lost.' Just so, I tell you, there will be more joy in heaven over one sinner who repents, than over nine-nine righteous persons who need no repentance. (Luke 15:1-7)

PRACTICAL

When my youngest son Collin was planning his wedding with Kim, he came to me and said he wanted to honor his mom at the wedding. I asked him what he had in mind. He said to simply have a place where she would sit, marked by a rose. For those who knew his mom, once they saw this empty seat and the rose, many began to weep. Her memory was with us that day. His brother Eric was his best man and told a story that involved his mother. And I did as well. We remembered and honored his mother in a special way on a special day.

In his 1917 paper, *Mourning and Melancholia*, Sigmund Freud posited that the sooner we *decathect*, or withdraw our emotional energy from our loved one, the sooner we would "recover" from our grief.[1] We know now, there are two things wrong with this theory. First, our love endures death. Our emotional attachment changes over time, but it is because we love that we grieve. Secondly, we don't recover from grief, we learn to assimilate our loss into our life's narrative. We hold room in our hearts for our loved one's memories, and in honoring their life, we can find meaning in ours. Frankl said, "Living in the past is meaningless, but honoring the past has meaning and purpose." Collin had ten years with his mother, who helped shape his life in innumerable ways. On his wedding day, he honored her love for him, because his love for her continues.

Grief Rituals

We perform rituals every day. We brush our teeth a certain way. We pray before each meal, "bless our Lord for these gifts…." Our morning coffee ritual. One of the ways that we remember and honor our loved ones is through the practice of grief rituals.

Grief rituals, to those who are engaged in them, are personal and intentionally meaningful events or ceremonies. They can be small or large, simple or complex. Studies tell us that grief rituals help us to gain back some sense of control in an otherwise uncontrollable world.

> ## REMEMBERING AND HONORING
>
> Remembering our loved ones means treasuring the gifts they left us with, the memories, the linking objects and how they helped to shape our lives. Simple rituals are meaningful expressions of love that help us transition to a new and different life.

According to Kenneth Doka,[2] rituals are designed to help us in four different ways:

1. Help us to have a continuing bond with our love one.
2. Help to signify that a transition is taking place.
3. Help us to reconcile the relationship.
4. Help us to affirm our love.

Continuing Bond Rituals

Continuing bond rituals help us to understand that the bonds forged in life are not destroyed by death. Love endures. These rituals help us to redefine the relationship and to remember back to the times that we shared together.

No ritual should be forced, but should fit the narrative of the life they lived.

One of our favorite continuing bond ritual stories comes from Carol and Marty. Their daughter Emma was only twenty-one when she died. Emma had been studying to be a primatologist—one who studies primates such as gorillas. A year or two after Emma died, Carol, Marty, and Emma's brothers and friends decided to honor Emma by participating in Denver's annual Gorilla Run. They all dressed in gorilla outfits and ran or walked the five kilometers. Although the event raises funds for the Mountain Gorilla Conservation Fund, that wasn't the main reason these people did this. They simply wanted to remember and honor a daughter, a sister and a friend; this run linked Emma back to them. Emma remains in their hearts and will always be loved.

Other examples of continuing bond rituals are:

- Candle lighting on a special day,
- Mass offering/prayer,
- Looking through old photo albums,
- Watching their favorite movie/listening to a favorite song,
- Baking their favorite meal or dessert,
- Attending a favorite sporting event,
- Commemorating a park bench in their honor and visiting it,
- Planting a tree and nourishing it.

Rituals of Transition

Rituals of transition mark a change that is taking place in the grieving process. Six years after her husband's death, a young widow found it unbearable to remove her wedding ring. A ritual was devised by her counselor (Dr. Doka) and her priest. At the end of Mass, she came up to the sanctuary. They recited her wedding vows in past tense. And after saying "until death did he part," the priest said to her, "May I have this ring?" She removed her ring for the first time in six years and then gave it to her priest.

This ritual marked that a transition had taken place. Her love for her husband was forever, but she was now ready and determined to chart a new course for her life, maybe even start dating again. The priest returned her ring. The woman had her ring linked with her husband's ring and framed with their wedding picture. This symbolized her vows had been completed.

Rituals of Reconciliation

Rituals of reconciliation help finish unfinished business. They help us to receive or extend forgiveness, and allow us to express thoughts and emotions, even after our loved one's death. For example, Sharon's husband and mother died within a few months of each other. During one of our workshops she raised her hand and asked, "I feel as though I am processing my husband's death, but not my mother's. What can I do?" Something was blocking Sharon from mourning her mother's death. What was it? Sandy and I believed it was some unresolved issues or conflict that was never dealt with before her mother died. Unresolved issues tend to stay unresolved, but not always. We suggested that Sharon write a letter to her mother. And in this letter, she was to get it all out. She was to tell her mother how she felt and how her mother may have made her feel. Sharon wrote that letter... five pages long! She folded it, put it in a sachet and buried it in her back yard, under a small statue of St. Jude. This simple ritual gave Sharon the liberation she needed to move forward and to mourn her mother's death. In burying the letter, she was also forgiving her mother, closing old wounds and letting them heal.

Soil Collection

In 1993 Bryan Stevenson started an organization called "The Equal Justice Initiative."[3] It's a legal advocacy group based in Montgomery, Alabama, that focuses on defending the rights of the poor and powerless. Stevenson has chronicled over 4,000 public lynchings of black men and women, most guilty only by association, not evidence. This is a period in our country's history that he calls "racial terror," in which after the Civil War, black people were given the right to vote, but public lynching was a brutal intimidation tactic that kept them clear of the voting booth, and kept white people in control.

To bring about reconciliation, Stevenson believes that the truth must be told, and the wrongs that took place years ago must be acknowledged. His research has identified the names of the persons who were lynched, and the date and approximate place that each killing took place. He finds descendants of each person and takes them out to the lynching site where they collect soil and place it in a glass jar. This is done to document and remember these people who truly died a slave's death; it ushers in some healing for their family and friends.

Rituals of Affirmation

Rituals of affirmation help to thank our loved ones for their love and the things they helped us with in our life. Nicole was only nine years old when she died. Her mother created "pay-it-forward" cards. She hands these cards out each week, asking people to do a random act of kindness in honor of her daughter, whose "legacy was kindness." This is a simple gesture, a random act of kindness, but it is her mother's way to honor and remember her daughter because Nicole was kind. In this way, Nicole is teaching others what it means to be kind. This ritual has great meaning for her mother, and is a way for her to stay connected with Nicole. Every time someone does something kind for someone else, this person is connected to Nicole as well. Nicole's legacy of kindness extends beyond her death.

The Elephant Whisperer

In 2012 Lawrence Anthony died. Who was Lawrence Anthony? Lawrence Anthony was a legend in South Africa. He was known as the "Elephant Whisperer."[4] He was a conservationist and environmentalist. He was known mostly though for saving hundreds of elephants from being brutally killed for their tusks. He lived with the elephants to gain their trust. He became one of them. When he died, a line of elephants, led by two matriarchs, marched twelve miles to Lawrence Anthony's house in South Africa. They remembered their way there from a journey three years earlier. We do not know for sure how they knew their friend had died. They hung around his house for two days. They didn't eat or drink. And after paying their respects they returned to their home. Elephants are known to mourn their own, but in this case, they mourned a human—their friend.

Maximillian Kolbe

Franciszek Gajowniczek is not a household name. Yet in 1940, he was the man Maximillian Kolbe[5] saved from being executed by the German soldiers in the Auschwitz death camp. Franciszek begged the soldiers, "don't take me, I have a wife and children." To which Kolbe responded, "I am a Catholic priest, I have no wife or children, take me instead of this man." The soldiers agreed, and Kolbe was later killed by lethal injection. Gajowniczek lived until the age of ninety-three. He is quoted as saying "it was my duty to tell people of the heroic act of love by Maximillian Kolbe." Gajowniczek was present with Pope John Paul II when Kolbe was both beatified and later canonized.

All Saints' and All Souls' Day Rituals

The Catholic ritual of honoring the saints is called All Saints' Day and occurs every November 1. This is a solemn Holy Day when we honor the saints who are believed to be in heaven. All Souls' Day occurs every November 2, when we pray for the beloved dead who die in a state of grace yet are in purgatory being cleansed of their sins. As Catholics, we believe that our prayers matter and can lift our beloved to heaven.

Day of the Dead

This ritual is celebrated in Mexico between October 31 and November 2. It is a festive celebration where the deceased loved ones are honored. During this time, Mexicans gather together, often adorning the graves with flowers and pictures. Family and friends share stories, often accompanied by song and dance.

Sitting Shiva and the Mourning Prayer

Sitting Shiva is a week-long Jewish ritual after the death of a loved one. The Hebrew word Shiva means "seven." The ritual is derived from the Book of Genesis. In chapter 50, Joseph mourned his father's death for seven days. At the funeral, mourners are given a ribbon to wear throughout Shiva. Immediately after the burial of a first-degree relative, people gather in one home and receive visitors, who are expected to bring food. During these visits, the mourners can share stories about the deceased. Mourners are expected to refrain from bathing during this mourning period.

In Jewish tradition, mourners also gather often during the first year and say Kaddish, the mourners' prayer. According to Jewish custom, the ongoing work of mourning lasts a lifetime.

Remembering and Honoring During the Holidays

For many who are grieving, the holidays and other special days can be very difficult. These times can be painful reminders of the past and what was. The people in the stores, family and friends, may be joyful, yet we are not. We may feel that no one else is even thinking about him or her, the person for whom we grieve. And then there is the whole issue of time. There is not enough of it, and with whom are we going to spend our time? And what about traditions? Do I need to host Christmas when I don't feel up to it?

"Grief Bursts" or STUGs (Sudden, Temporary, Upsurges in Grief) are very common during the holidays, especially in the first year or two after our loved one's death. It is when we are seemingly doing fine that a grief burst will hit us. They usually come on suddenly and are triggered by something, maybe a song, a scent, a site, a word or even a scene. They usually last a minute or two and then are gone until the next one.

Grieving during the holidays is difficult. We feel forced to fit some joy inside our pain. We don't want to disappoint other people, but at the same time, we are not ourselves. Here are some tips to navigate the holidays.

Be somewhat selfish:

- Listen to your body and take care of yourself.
- If you need some alone time, take it.
- Go to a movie.
- Pamper yourself a little.
- Light a candle and be still.
- Go for a walk.
- Take an afternoon nap.
- Go to lunch with a friend.

Develop a simple plan and communicate it to others:

- Other people need to know your intentions for these holidays.
- Don't feel obligated to attend every function or gathering.
- It's okay to say "no."
- Communicate your plans to others.

Take time to remember your loved one:

- Remember, others might not know how to "approach your grief."

- If you do attend a party, ask whether it would be alright to take a few minutes to share stories. You might be surprised to get a few laughs as well as tears.

- If you host a party, you could ask people to come prepared with their favorite story to share with others.

- You could also remember your loved one by making their favorite dish or baked goods.

- Include an empty chair at the table.

- Buy gifts that you imagine your loved one would have bought for you or others.

- Look through photo albums together. Only do this if you are up to it. If you cry, you cry. If you laugh, you laugh. It's all part of the process.

- Create a "Memory Album." Every holiday Sandy reads memories and stories from a collection that she gathered for Morgan and Ryan. It is a time of laughter and tears.

Start a new tradition:

- If you were always the "host," ask someone else to host.

- Bake your favorite pie.

- Instead of Christmas ornaments, tie pictures of your loved one on the tree.

Summary

Remembering and honoring our loved ones is an important part of the mourning process. Connecting ourselves to those whom we have loved and lost, through memories and storytelling, is healing. Anytime we break open, we avoid breaking down. In remembering and honoring, we go where we must go. When we face the fear of grief, what is looking back at us, is always love. There are lessons to be learned from everyone's life. When we honor a life lived, we learn more about what those lessons were, how they might help us and others, and how we create meaning from all of this.

PERSONAL

Questions to reflect on:

What ritual can you implement?

Is there any unfinished business you need to finish?

What lessons can you learn from your loved one's life?

Works of Mercy: Feed the Hungry

On the next Thanksgiving consider volunteering to help those who have nothing to eat on this day. Perhaps a soup kitchen or your church-sponsored event to feed the homeless. Do this in honor of your loved one.

Take some quiet time to write...

Your Second Intention: Remember and Honor

It is my intention to...

NOTES

1. Sigmund Freud, "Mourning and Melancholia." Essay. *The Standard Edition of Complete Psychological Works of Sigmund Freud*, Vol XIV. (The Hogarth Press, 1914-1916) pp. 243-58.

2. Dr. Kenneth Doka, *Grief Counseling Resource Guide*. New York State Office of Mental Health, 2004.

3. Bryan Stevenson, *Equal Justice Initiative*. CBS 60 Minutes broadcast, 8 April 2018, eji.org.

4. Protect All Wildlife, *When the Elephants Came to Mourn Lawrence Anthony*. YouTube (https://www.youtube.com/watch?v=Tjp_nPRtCLo&t=207s), 31 May 2017.

5. Maximilian Kolbe, Wikipedia, https://en.wikipedia.org/wiki/Maximilian_Kolbe, accessed 26 October 2018.

 THOMAS MERTON

In a world of tension and breakdown it is necessary for there to be those who seek to integrate their inner lives not by avoiding anguish and running away from problems, but by facing them in their naked reality and their ordinariness.

CHAPTER 5

The Third Intention: Acceptance

PRAYERFUL

Father, if you are willing, remove this chalice from me; nevertheless, not my will but yours be done. (Luke 22:42)

Let us pray. *In the name of the Father, and of the Son and the Holy Spirit.*

O God, grant me the serenity to accept the things I cannot change, the courage to change the things I can, and the wisdom to know the difference. Living one day at a time, enjoying one moment at a time. Accepting hardships as the pathway to peace. Taking, as He did, the sinful world as it is, not as I would have it. Trusting that He will make all things right if I surrender to His will; that I may be reasonably happy in this life, and supremely happy with Him forever.

Elizabeth Ann Seton, pray for us.

Peter's Denial Foretold

"Truly I say to you, this very night, before the cock crows twice, you will deny me three times." But he (Peter) said vehemently, "If I must die with you, I will not deny you." And they all said the same. And they went to a place which was called Gethsemane; and he said to his disciples, "sit here while I pray. And he took with him Peter and James and John, and began to be greatly distressed and troubled. And he said to them, my soul is sorrowful, even to death; remain here and watch. And going a little farther, he fell on the ground and prayed that if it were possible, the hour might pass from him. And he said, "Abba, Father, all things are possible to you; remove this chalice from me; yet not what I will, but what you will." (MARK 14:30-36)

After Peter's betrayal and the subsequent arrest of Jesus, Peter followed Jesus "from a distance" into the courtyard. Within a span of about one hour, three people noticed Peter and accused him of knowing Jesus. All three times, just as Christ foretold, Peter denied knowing his friend. "Man, I do not know what you are saying." (LUKE 22:60)

PRACTICAL

Why does Peter deny Christ? Fear is what often leads us into a protective posture. Peter, though his love for Christ was real, was not yet fully convinced or accepting that Jesus would do what he proclaimed that he would do, that is, suffer, die and rise again on the third day. Peter feared for his life. So we see Peter in all kinds of "distressing disguises," denying that he knows Jesus, to save his own life.

Contrary to Peter, Christ was accepting of his mission, that he must suffer, die, and rise again on the third day. Peter objects to this mission and will not hear of his Lord having to suffer. "God forbid, Lord!" To which Jesus admonishes Peter, telling him, "Get behind me, Satan! You are not on the side of God, but of men" (MATT 16:22-23). In the Garden of Gethsemane, Peter drew his sword only to have Jesus tell him to put his sword back. Jesus was again accepting his fate. And in praying to his Father, he said, "not as I will, but as you will."

With any situation that we face, we have three options. We can accept the situation as it is, we can alter it in some way, or we can avoid it altogether. If while driving we notice a vibration that wasn't happening a few seconds earlier, we can no longer alter or avoid the reality that we have a flat tire. We accept that our back-right tire is flat and then we act. We can

> **ACCEPTANCE**
>
> Through acceptance we come to terms with what has happened. It is felt in our hearts and interpreted by our minds. Acceptance does not alleviate our suffering, but it does allow us to begin the journey to create meaning and purpose in our suffering.

either change the tire ourself, call for assistance, wait for a good Samaritan to come by and help us, or we can call a taxi. If while traveling on the highway and a deer comes out of the darkness, we alter our course as quickly and safely as possible, to avoid hitting the deer. If we are allergic to poison ivy, we should do our best to avoid it.

> The way in which a man accepts his fate and the suffering it entails, the way in which he takes up his cross, gives him ample opportunity—even under the most difficult circumstances—to add meaning to his life. Everywhere man is confronted with fate, with the chance of achieving something, through his own suffering.[1]

We suffer when we resist or oppose what is real. "The more one longs for something, the more pain does deprivation of it become" (ST. THOMAS AQUINAS). This is not to say that we should not have an emotional reaction to what is. If someone harms us, our reaction might be anger, and we shouldn't resist being angry. Allow it to happen. Feelings are usually truthful. They are neutral in that they are neither right nor wrong; they are what they are. Our behavior on the other hand *can* be right or wrong.

St. Paul writes,

> Be angry, but do not sin; do not let the sun go down
> on your anger and give no opportunity for the devil.
> (Eph 4:26-27)

Denial

To understand acceptance, we must first understand its antithesis. Denial is a refusal to accept the truth in order to avoid anxiety and discomfort. It's a defense mechanism to protect ourselves from a reality that seems overwhelming. It's been called "emotional anesthesia." It is commonly found in three situations: addiction, sexual trauma, and loss of a loved one (grief). When we are in a state of denial about something, we are fighting the truth in an exhausting attempt to mitigate the reality of what we must face.

Denial is a coping instrument. By not allowing too much in, we give ourselves some space and time to absorb what has happened. In small measured doses, denial is healthy. It protects us from more than we can handle at that time.

Remember that we have three choices in all circumstances: accept, alter, or avoid. When it comes to the loss of a loved one, until there is acceptance of this loss, with both heart and mind, there is a separation to endure, yet nothing to mourn. Denial or suppression diminishes our response to act and they exhaust us as we work harder and harder to suppress our emotions.

With grief, there are two primary ways that we use denial: we deny the facts of what has happened, or we downplay the significance of the relationship of who has died.

Denial of the Facts

Denial of the facts can range from a bending of the truth to a full-blown delusion. When we bend the truth, we are trying to re-shape what happened into a narrative that fits what we want to believe. For example, we may want to believe that our daughter died from an accidental drug overdose, when all the objective evidence points to suicide. We may refuse to accept the facts as they are; rather we reconstruct another story that is plausible, yet not likely.

Downplay the Significance

To downplay the significance is to deny the meaning or importance of who the person was who died. "We weren't close," is a common phrase heard. When we modulate the relationship, we minimize what the loss means to us, forming this protective barrier around our heart. An exhausting attempt to prove we are something we are not, as if it will change who we are.

Suppression

Suppression is a close cousin to denial. Suppression is a conscious decision to avoid or delay action. Women tend to suppress anger. Men tend to be good at suppressing sadness. About 75% of people with addiction issues have suffered from previous trauma in their life. Trauma is a broad term to describe many things, some of which could be sexual abuse, death of a close relative or friend, accident, war, neglect and many others. Rather than face the source of the trauma, they choose to suppress or soften their belief in what happened. This painful wound, no matter how bad, if not confronted and processed, will only fester and worsen as it ages. By avoiding what really happened, the addict self-medicates to bury the pain even deeper.

When delusional, one maintains a fixed, false and often bizarre belief that resists correction, despite overwhelming evidence. A delusional person cannot process logic and often misinterprets perceptions or experiences. The situation they are in is either not real or highly exaggerated.

> Christ does not answer directly, and he does not answer in the abstract this human questioning about the meaning of suffering. Man hears Christ's saving answer as he himself gradually becomes a sharer in the sufferings of Christ.[2]

Christ accepted His mission and through His suffering and death, surrendered everything back to the Father.

Acceptance is not to be confused with the fifth stage of grief from Elisabeth Kübler-Ross. Acceptance is not passive; it requires our active participation and full intention. When it comes to grief and loss, our minds tend to move towards acceptance of what happened and then away from it or suppressing it. But, before the mourning process can begin, we must accept and acknowledge, on both an emotional and cognitive level, what has happened.

Acceptance is necessary for us to assimilate this loss into the narrative of our life. Although our mind knows that death is permanent, this intention deals with more than just the finality of death.

We must come to accept four things.

1. Who we have lost (parent, spouse, child, relative, friend);

2. What we have lost (plans, dreams, goals, hopes and other secondary losses);

3. Who we now are (widowed, orphaned, "only parent," a couple who has lost a child);

4. What remains of this relationship (How do we have an enduring connection?).

Who We Have Lost and How They Died

It cannot be emphasized enough how grief is as unique as our fingerprint. Losing a parent who was ninety-three and suffered with Alzheimer's for ten years, will be accepted differently than the sudden death of a twenty-one-year-old child. One was anticipated for some time. The other was unexpected. When we can anticipate our loss, acceptance settles over us gradually, giving us time to adjust and make plans. But when our loss is sudden, acceptance is forced upon us abruptly; there is no time to adjust, and plans are forced on us.

So, who we lost and how they died affects our ability to understand and accept what happened. With a sudden loss—such as an accident, a completed suicide, or homicide—one moment they are here, and then they are gone. A sense of disbelief, shock and numbness frequently accompanies this type of loss and may last for some time. There is little time to plan anything. It's as if we have been hit by a tsunami and are trying to find our bearings of where we are, what has happened and how we are going to surface so that we can breathe again. We may struggle with acceptance as we struggle with everything else.

> Our family's Catholic faith was tested by a raging fire the night my husband and I stood at our front door and received news that our dear son Thomas has

taken his life. Up until that day our family lived in what many in our community thought was the perfect Catholic family. Though Thomas was suffering from depression and drug use, we kept this mostly hidden behind a shadow of denial, praying he would get better. The slow and painful process of purification began when the truth was revealed. Our hearts were raw and empty for the world to see. 'What do you want from me, Lord?' was the look we all wore after his death. Like the Apostles locked in the Upper Room, hiding in fear after their Lord was gone, so too our family remained, shut in, full of grief and confusion. Yet it was only days later, when I witnessed my daughters comforting our grieving community, that it seemed Jesus had come into our midst telling us, *Be not afraid.* My husband broke the stigma of silence by heroically standing at his funeral..., talking about Thomas' struggles, urging parents to talk openly to their kids about drug use. From this witness other families have come forward, uncovering their shame to seek help for their children. The death of our son has taught us that a more perfect Catholic family leaves no traces of shadows but embraces the cross of Christ in the Light of truth. —Anne Redlinger.[3]

What We Have Lost

The question we often ask ourselves is, why? Why did he get cancer? Why is this happening to me now? Why didn't I do something? Why is life so unfair? Why did she take her life? Why didn't I protect her? Why does God allow suffering? Why? Why? Why?

The death of a loved one brings secondary losses of dreams, hopes and plans, which must be accepted as well. If we are widowed, and depending on our relative age, the secondary losses could include, lost retirement years, loss of co-grandparenting, loss of seeing children graduate, getting married, having children or more children and having careers. If we lose a young child, we have similar secondary losses, such as graduations, weddings, careers and watching children become parents themselves. When we lose one parent, we not only grieve for ourselves, but we feel for the surviving parent.

Events, such as births, graduations and weddings may trigger emotions, or bursts of grief. A young bride may be tearful on her wedding day, if her father isn't there to walk her down the aisle and dance the daddy-daughter dance. A grandfather may be emotional on the birth of a grandchild, knowing that his wife isn't there to share in his joy.

Immaculée Ilibagiza spent ninety-one days during the Rwandan genocide huddled with seven other women in a cramped bathroom. She prayed every waking moment. When it was finally over, she discovered that her entire family had been brutally murdered by the Hutu extremists. She wrote,

> We all shared in the misery that had descended upon the village, but I knew that the people gathered around me had lost much more than I had. They'd lost their faith—and in doing so, they'd lost hope. I stared at the coffins of my mother and Damascene and thought of my father and Vianney, whose bodies I would never recover....and I thanked God. I may have lost everything, but I'd kept my faith, and it made me strong. It also comforted me and let me know that life still held purpose.[4]

Who We Are Now

This is about accepting not only who we are now but accepting the new roles that we may now have in our life. After Sandy and I were each widowed at a young age, we unwittingly became "only-parents." We were both mother and father to our children. I had a career and a job that was quite demanding. My boys were still too young to be on their own, which meant that I had to make plans when I traveled. Sandy stayed home for a while, but she went back to work too and had to make similar arrangements. We both had to be the primary emotional support to our children who lost their mother and father.

During 9/11, I was in Utah at a national sales meeting. The country fell into chaos. Air travel was forbidden. I and several of my colleagues drove an RV across the country to get home. I drove the last leg of the journey. It took twenty-nine hours! Although the boys were with their grandparents, I remember having this tremendous maternal instinct to get home, to give them a big hug and to make sure they were safe. I was in that moment both mother and father.

The Power of Our Minds

We all live dualistic lives. There is our life outside our body, the things we do every day, our routines, our jobs, our habits. And then there is our life inside our minds. The stories we keep telling ourselves and the roles we play in these stories. Are we heroes or victims? The protagonists or the antagonist?

Pessimists doubt that they will succeed, and that everything is global and permanent; optimists doubt that anything will go wrong, and everything is temporary and transient. Denying that we will succeed is literally telling our brain to withhold the resources we need to succeed. I'm somewhat of an expert on this. When I'm at the gym, if I don't prepare myself for a good workout—if I don't give myself goals to achieve—my workout is doomed. I'll start telling myself, "I can't." Then my brain will start conserving my energy for something it believes I *can* do. Negative programing of our minds will inevitably create negative experiences in our lives. Conversely, if my mindset is positive and I have goals to achieve, my brain will supply the necessary energy to accomplish these goals.

Has anything happened exactly as you planned it? Of course not. The weather changes. Something gets canceled at the last minute. If we deny that anything can go wrong, then we will never prepare for the unexpected things that will inevitably cross our paths.

Grief needs neither pessimism nor optimism, it requires a realistic acceptance of what-is. We can crawl slowly and intentionally towards the light, or we can remain in the darkness. But this is always our choice. How we feel today is how we feel today. But it doesn't mean that we will feel this way a month from now or a year from now. Death is permanent and inevitable, but so is (please God) eternity. All else is dust. Accept this moment for what it is. Face each challenge as it comes. Hold on to the hope that you will get through this.

There was an experiment performed in Japan that involved thirteen students, all of whom were allergic to poison ivy.[5] One arm of each was exposed to a harmless plant, but the students were told that the plant was poison ivy. All thirteen students broke out in a rash.

The other arm was exposed to poison ivy, but they were told it was a harmless plant. Only two of the thirteen students broke out in a rash. This experiment points out the amazing power of our minds. The students' beliefs alone were enough to make each of them have a physical reaction, when no such reaction should have occurred. Why is this? What we keep telling ourselves, through our internal monologue, has a huge effect on our physical and mental health. Psychologists call this "Expectancy Theory." Our brains can create patterns that mimic the real world. So, in other words, the *expectation* of an event happening causes the brain to react *as if the event was really happening*. This triggers our central nervous system and can lead to many potential physical reactions, in this case, a rash associated with poison ivy.

We have thousands of thoughts every day. Most are repetitive; many are useless. Some are harmful. When we are under stress, our thoughts become increasingly negative. Under stress, our bodies are in a constant "fight or flight" mode, which puts our minds in the same mode too. Our minds invent stories, trying to make some sense of what is happening. This repetitive negative thinking not only changes the physical architecture of our brain, but also clouds out reality. We begin to believe that what we are thinking is real.

We all have movies we enjoy and love to watch them repeatedly, maybe around Christmas with a big bowl of popcorn. We know the words that each actor will say. We know each scene and how it will unfold. We know the arc of the story, yet still we watch with total wonder as if it's our first time. We laugh. We cry. Then there are the movies that we loathe. These movies give us a visceral reaction when just the title is mentioned. We never watch these movies again, do we? No. Why? Because we have a choice: watch or not watch.

Such is the case with our minds. We may not always have a choice about what goes into our minds, yet we do have a choice of the tape that we keep playing in our minds on a continuous loop—in a word, rumination. This tape is the bad movie that we loathe, and which if given the choice would never watch again. Yet we keep playing this tape; we even rewind it so that in case we missed something, we are able to experience the madness again.

Thinking without some awareness of what we keep telling ourselves can be maddening. We need to be keenly aware of what we keep telling ourselves. Internal monologue is much like digestion and breathing: it happens and we don't notice it. Yet what we keep telling ourselves plays an important role in our physical and mental health. Depression is largely the result of faulty thinking, where negatives override the positives. This faulty thinking physically changes our brain. But once we begin to change the way we think, our brain changes too.

If the tape in one's mind keeps playing a repetitive and negative script, this script can become real, as we saw with the poison ivy experiment. If we keep telling ourselves that we can't accomplish something, we are telling our brain to withhold resources. But when we quiet our mind, we often find the stories that we have been telling ourselves are mostly fictional. We have the power to change the narrative and let go of the fictional stories that will never happen.

Mindfulness Prayer

Let's face it, we do many daily activities on automatic pilot. We have habits and our daily routines. My first thing every morning is to come downstairs and reach for my first cup of coffee, which sprung to life on a timer because I didn't want to wait a few minutes for it to brew. My feet know the way to the coffee. My hands know the way. My taste buds know the way. I don't have to think about any of it. So my mind is away, thinking about what I will do after I get my first sip of coffee in me. I am not in this moment. I am in a future moment and then I'm on to another future moment before the last moment ever ends. I'm not mindful of anything, I'm mindless of everything. My body is doing one thing, while my mind is somewhere else.

Mindfulness means our minds and bodies are experiencing sameness with focused attention to what is happening now. We allow all our senses to work in harmony with each other. The morning routine looks and feels different. We notice things, such as how it feels when our feet touch the floor. We say a prayer of gratefulness for another day. We feel our hand turning the doorknob. On the walk downstairs, we notice things we don't normally notice, we see the pictures on the walls, the smiles on people's faces. We feel the house getting warmer as the furnace comes to life, we see the darkness that engulfs the house. We smell the aroma of the coffee. We feel our fingers grabbing the handle of the coffee mug. We listen to the sound as coffee pours into the mug. We hear a cardinal singing, the breeze blowing, the rain falling. We are one with the moment, in complete acceptance as it is. And we are grateful for all of it.

Mindfulness helps us to bring our ever-escaping minds that want to focus on what was or what could be and gets them to focus on what is. We don't run from our problems, we see them for what they truly are, and not what our minds tell us they are, which is usually fiction and complete rubbish.

Mindfulness Prayer helps us get out of our thinking mind— "Nothing pleases God more than a mind free of all occupations and distractions" (ALBERT MAGNUS)—and into an awareness mind; and what is prayer if it is not an awareness of the presence of God? St. Paul tells us to "rejoice always, pray constantly, give thanks in all circumstances, for this is the will of God in Christ Jesus for you" (1 THESS 5:16-18). In Mindfulness Prayer we express every moment in prayerful gratitude. We slowly suspend the tension of fear and anxiety. We are in the boat. The boat is in the storm. We are not so much grateful for the storm and the suffering it brings, but we are grateful for the boat. Because even though Christ is asleep in the boat, He is in the boat with us. Eventually He'll calm the seas, yet in this moment, we are held in His hands. In this moment we are safe.

> And when He (Jesus) got in the boat, His disciples followed Him. And behold, there arose a great storm on the sea, so the boat was being swamped by the waves; but He was asleep. And they went and woke Him saying, "save us Lord; we are perishing." And He said to them, "why are you afraid, O men of little faith?" Then He arose and rebuked the winds and the sea, and there was great calm (MATT 8:23-26).

For our honeymoon in November 2009, Sandy and I booked a cruise that departed from Tampa Bay, Florida. Yes, November is still hurricane season and yes, Hurricane Ida was prowling about the Gulf of Mexico as we were about to depart. Some cruise ships went out and turned back. Not ours! We went out and into the backlash of this storm. The first night the seas were twenty-five feet. Ever been in twenty-foot swells? You don't want to be. The clanging wine glasses in our room and the scary rocking of the ship was enough for me to know it's bad out there—don't look! But Sandy did look outside our balcony view. She saw the waves. Thank goodness we took our sea sickness pills.

The next night at the Captain's Dinner, we took our sea-weary legs, sleepless eyes and anxiety-filled minds up to the captain to ask what his thinking was, taking us into such peril. His response was priceless. With a smile, he said something like this, "I know what I'm doing. This ship can handle seas far worse than this. You let me take care of the waves."

Isn't that what Christ is telling us? Isn't He saying, I may lead you into some storms to test your faith, "In this world you will have trouble," but let Me lead you through the storms, "but be of good cheer, I have overcome the world" (JOHN 16:33). Put your faith in Me, the one who redeemed you, who through my suffering, paid the price for you. Take your minds off things that you can't control, the waves, the sea, the winds. Let all that stuff go. Calm yourself and focus your attention back to Me. Listen for Me. "Take up your cross and follow Me" (MATT 16:24). "Be still and know that I am God" (Ps 46:10). Be aware and grateful for the beauty that surrounds you. Do not run from storms, but rather hold tight to My garment and I will lead you through the storms.

Anxiety is fueled by thoughts of either the past or the future. "And which of you by being anxious can add one cubit to his span of life?" (MATT 6:27). If an expectant mother is always anxious, it will affect her unborn child. The same is true of our grief, our pain and our suffering. If we don't transform it, we will transmit it, both inwardly against ourselves, and outwardly towards others. But when we stop the endless thinking, rethinking and ruminating we take our minds out of the endless spin cycle, and increase our awareness on what is happening right now. What is happening right now is within our control, including our thoughts. According to St. Francis de Sales:

> Never be in a hurry, do everything quietly and in a calm spirit. Do not lose your inner peace for anything whatsoever, even if your world seems upset.[6]

Pope Francis said we spend too much time thinking about ourselves and not enough time with God. Pray. Be still. Quiet our minds. What stories are you telling yourself? Are they true? Are they helping or hurting you?

Summary

Acceptance is an important part of the grief process. We cannot change what we don't acknowledge and accept for what it is. At first, for some of us, denial is a natural defense mechanism that protects our hearts and insulates us from too much pain. But denial is meant to be a short-term solution to a longer-term situation. Often our storytelling minds can hinder our progress. We must be mindful of what we keep telling ourselves. We are not what we *think*, we are what we *do*. Accepting our pain and the truth of our situation, allows us to begin the journey, to act.

PERSONAL

Questions to reflect on:

What things are you still hesitant to accept?

Has denial helped or hurt you? Explain.

How can you quiet your mind?

Works of Mercy: Comfort the Sorrowful

Consider doing something to help someone else who is grieving. Attend Mass together. Go out for lunch and just listen. Write them a note. Do this in honor of your loved one.

Take some quiet time to write...

Your Third Intention: Acceptance

It is my intention...

NOTES

1. Viktor E. Frankl, *Man's Search for Meaning*. (Boston Mass.: Beacon Press, 2006).

2. St. Pope John Paul II, *Salvifici Doloris* (*On the Christian Meaning of Human Suffering*). 11 February 1984. http://w2.vatican.va/content/john-paul-ii/en/apost_letters/1984/documents/hf_jp-ii_apl_11021984_salvifici-doloris.html. §26.

3. Anne Redlinger, "Be Not Afraid." (reflection) *Magnificat* (San Diego, Cal.: 3 February 2018) p. 138. Originally appeared in Dom. Roberto, ER. CAM. *From The Love of Mary*. (Charlotte, NC: Tan Books [www.tanbooks.com], 1984).

4. Immaculée Ilibagiza, *Left To Tell*, (Hay House Publishing, 2014).

5. Shawn Achor, *The Happiness Advantage*, (Crown Business, 2010).

6. St. Francis de Sales, as quoted on ThinkExists.com, http://thinkexist.com/quotation/never_be_in_a_hurry-do_everything_quietly_and_in/14806.html, accessed 26 October 2018.

 ## ST. JOHN PAUL II

The reality of suffering is ever before our eyes and often in our body, soul, and heart of each of us. Pain has always been a great riddle of human existence. However, ever since Jesus redeemed the world by His passion and death, a new perspective has been opened; through suffering one can grow in self-giving and attain the highest degree of love because of Him who "loved us and gave Himself up for us.

CHAPTER 6

The Fourth Intention: Yield to the Pain

PRAYERFUL

When Jesus saw her weeping and the Jews came with her also weeping, He was deeply moved in spirit and troubled; and He said, "where have you laid him?" And they said, "Lord, come and see." Jesus wept. (JOHN 11:33-35)

Let us pray. *In the name of the Father, and of the Son and the Holy Spirit.*

Lord Jesus, help me to trust in your unwavering love and saving help, especially when I meet adversities, trials and temptations. Give me your peace when I am troubled and let me know the joy of your victory over sin and death.

Elizabeth Ann Seton, pray for us.

The Parable of the Prodigal Son

A man had two sons. And the younger of them said to his father, "Father, give me the share of property that is coming to me." And he divided his property between them. Not many days later, the younger son gathered all he had and took a journey into a far country, and there he squandered his property in reckless living. And when he had spent everything, a severe famine arose in that country, and he began to be in need. So, he went and hired himself out to one of the citizens of that country, who sent him into his fields to feed pigs. And he was longing to be fed with the pods that the pigs ate, and no one gave him anything.

But when he came to himself, he said, "How many of my father's hired servants have more than enough bread, but I perish here with hunger! I will arise and go to my father, and I will say to him, 'Father, I have sinned against heaven and before you. I am no longer worthy to be called your son. Treat me as one of your hired servants.'" And he arose and came to his father. But while he was still a long way off, his father saw him and felt compassion, and ran and embraced him and kissed him. And the son said to him, "Father, I have sinned against heaven and before you. I am no longer worthy to be called your son." But the father said to his servants, "Bring quickly the best robe, and put it on him, and put a ring on his hand, and shoes on his feet. And bring the fattened calf and kill it and let us eat and celebrate. For this my son was dead, and is alive again; he was lost, and is found." And they began to celebrate.

Now his older son was in the field, and as he came and drew near to the house, he heard music and dancing. And he called one of the servants and asked what these things meant. And he said to him, "Your brother has come, and your father has killed the fattened calf, because he has received him back safe and sound." But he was angry and refused to go in. His father came out and entreated him, but he answered his father, "Look, these many years I have served you, and I never disobeyed your command, yet you never gave me a young goat, that I might celebrate with my friends. But when this son of yours came, who has devoured your property with prostitutes, you killed the fattened calf for him!" And he said to him, "Son, you are always with me, and all that is mine is yours. It was fitting to celebrate and be glad, for this your brother was dead, and is alive; he was lost, and is found." (LUKE 15:11-32)

PRACTICAL

T
o a first-century Jew, the cross was no laughing matter. The worst of the worst criminals were crucified by the Romans on crosses that weighed about 300 pounds. It was an ex-cruciatingly painful death. The person was tied to the cross and then seven-inch nails were pounded through the hands, wrists and feet and into the wooden beams. They were left there hanging for days until they died from asphyxiation, dehydration or pure exhaustion. *"Christianity is the only major religion to have as its central focus the suffering and degradation of its God."*[1]

What did Jesus mean when He said, "take up your cross and follow me?" This passage is found in three of the four gospels, and according to Fr. James Martin,[2] it means accepting that suffering is a part of our lives. The cross represents this suffering. We must come to terms with the fact that frustration, disappointment, pain, grief, sorrow, illness and death are part of living and are the crosses we must carry.

In the Old Testament, suffering and evil are synonymous with each other. In other words, we suffer when we sin. We see this expressed in the book of Job. Job was a "blameless and upright man, without fault," and suffered greatly with loss of possessions, sons and daughters and his own health. His own friends tried to convince Job that his trials were the just punishment for his apparent sin. In the book of Job we see suffering as justice, even though with Job himself there was no perniciousness at all.

Suffering has meaning as a form of punishment when there is sin.

But in Job's case there was no sin. Pope St. John Paul II writes, "not all suffering is a consequence of a fault and has the nature of punishment."

Acute physiological pain is a signal to stop what we are doing and change course. For example, we feel pain when we inadvertently place our hand on a hot stove. The pain tells our brain to remove our hand from the source from which the pain is coming. It is then that we address our wounds. Our hand will eventually heal.

YIELD TO THE PAIN

Yield to the pain means that we acknowledge and face our moral and physical suffering to fully grieve our loss. We swim with the current, our present situation.

With moral or psychological pain, removing ourselves from the source of our pain doesn't work. Trying to remove ourselves or the source of our pain is a form of denial in which neither ourselves nor the pain go anywhere. Nothing is solved, and nothing heals.

Moral pain is the emotional anguish that we experience, from wide-ranging causes, including, but not limited to the death of a loved one. As Pope St. John Paul II writes in his letter on suffering, *Salvifici Doloris*, "Man suffers whenever he experiences any kind of evil," which he describes evil as limitation, distortion or deprivation of good."[3]

Expressions of Grief

I just gave you a hanging mobile, the kind you might find over a baby's crib. I labeled the pieces to your mobile and they represent your life. Your cognitive style. Your current emotional state. Your daily routines. Your social relationships and family. Your physical body and health. Your job. Your finances. Your faith. These pieces, your life, are connected. Try having good social relationships if you're always yelling at people. Try having good finances without good income. Try having faith without belief. Now try hitting one of these pieces, just one, without the other pieces moving. Impossible right? When one moves, they all move in unpredictable ways. This is how grief affects every aspect of our life.

Grief is a *somatic* experience—it affects the whole body. Whatever affects us emotionally, will have a physiological signature, and whatever affects us physically, will likewise affect us emotionally. Physical suffering has boundaries, and with pain medications can be somewhat controlled. Moral suffering and that which affects one's mind, may not cause us physical pain, but that does not mean that it is not painful.

Emotions and Feelings

Emotions and feelings are often used interchangeably, but they are two distinct processes. Emotions come from the subcortical region of the brain, think amygdala, fight or flight. Or in other words, the "downstairs" brain. Emotional reactions are coded in our genes and are commonly similar with all of us. Emotions are instinctual. They are subconscious bodily reactions to a physical experience. Because of their physical nature, they can be measured in various ways, including brain activity, heart rate, facial expressions and body language.

Feelings come from the prefrontal cortex, or "upstairs" brain. Neuroscientist Antonio Damasio describes feelings as conscious reactions, expressed in thoughts. "Feelings are mental experiences of bodily states, which arise as the brain interprets emotions."[4] "Emotions play out in the theatre of our body, feelings play out in the theatre of our mind."[5] Feelings are influenced by our personal experiences, memories and belief systems. So, unlike emotions, feelings vary greatly from person to person.

Understanding emotions and feelings helps us to understand how we experience life, both joyous and difficult times.

To illustrate the difference between emotions and feelings, let's say you are flying on a three-hour business trip—coach class—to Orlando, Florida. There is an eight-year-old boy with Mickey Mouse ears sitting unattended in the seat behind you. Once in flight, the child begins to hit the back of your seat with his feet. Your head bobs back and forth. It's imperceptible at first, but your blood pressure slowly increases, as does your heart rate. Your cortisol level rises. Your facial expression changes to that of Ebenezer Scrooge. This is your subconscious emotional reaction to a physical stimulus—experienced in your body.

Then your mind begins to interpret what is happening. Feelings get expressed into thoughts. "This is annoying!" "I'm feeling angry!" "I can't let this continue the whole flight, I have work to do!" Already, your prefrontal cortex, where feelings originate, is helping you to navigate your way through this situation. They are urging you to confront, to act—to make a choice, to gain back control. You could hope that he stops while you ruminate about this little brat. You could let him to continue and let your anger bubble over into a semi-catatonic rage. Or, you could calmly talk with him and ask him to stop. If that doesn't work, you could talk with his parent or a flight attendant. Hopefully he then stops, and your anger is defused. Or is it? Do you let this incident ruminate with you the whole flight and beyond?

Feelings happen to us, yet we have the power to control how we respond to them. We can choose not to become our feelings. "You have two choices," wrote Rebecca Kowalski, whose seven-year-old son Chase died in the Sandy Hook shooting, "I could be in the bottom of a bottle; I could not get out of bed. Or, I could do what's making us heal a little bit every day."[6]

Until the last twenty years or so, emotions were viewed by cognitive experts as interruptions that got in the way of our mental processes; they interfered with reasoning, rather than assist in it. Emotions, we once thought, only occur when our behavior needed to be interrupted or altered. In addition, the assertion was that emotions had no physiological signature. Happiness and anger "felt" the same, but it was our cognitive interpretation (feelings) of our bodily response that distinguished these emotions from one another.

So, grief is first experienced as an emotional reaction, felt in our body, as we gather information through our senses. We *hear*. We *see*. We *touch*. Depending on the circumstances, these bodily changes will be similar. The change in our facial expression, the change in our posture, the gait in our walk, the dwindling energy level. Still many other changes are felt in our body yet may only be noticed by ourselves.

Then, as our brain begins to interpret all that is happening, the sequence evolves. Whereas emotions are an instantaneous reaction, memories from years ago play a role in the development of feelings, making feelings more differentiated and lasting. Awakened memories trigger nostalgic feelings expressed in thoughts. "I feel so sad." "There was nothing I could do to help." "I am angry because he left me alone." "I regret not having done more." "Now that she is gone, what will I do?" "How will I go on?" "Why did this happen?"

Our brain is the nerve center of our consciousness, and the most important contributing factor to our physical health is our emotional health. All emotions serve a purpose, so in that sense, there are no negative emotions. Anger should cause us to approach the source of our anger. Fear should cause us to remove ourselves or protect ourselves from the source of the fear. Fear often gets us to act in a smart way, without having to think.

According to Richard Davidson, PhD,[7] we need to look at emotions four different ways. An emotional state is ephemeral, lasting only a minute or two. A mood may last a few hours or a day. An emotional trait can last for years and is more defining of who we are—think serious, joyful, grouchy. Our emotional style is how we respond to life's experiences.

Emotional Style

Through methodical scientific experimentation, Davidson concluded that there are six dimensions to Emotional Style.

Resilience—How we respond to adversity. Are we crippled by it, or do we respond with determination to get through it?

Outlook—Is our outlook more positive or negative? Do we maintain a high level of energy even when things are not going our way?

Social Intuition—How well do we read body language? One's tone of voice?

Self-Awareness—How well are we aware of our own thoughts and feelings? Are we attuned to what our body is telling us?

Context—How appropriate is our behavior in social settings?

Attention—How well do we stay focused?

We all have elements of each of these and we need each to flourish. In addition, there is no right or wrong style. However, all of us are on a continuum with each style; we can score either quite low or quite high in each style. For example, scoring high in resilience tends to mean we will recover from setbacks faster than others who score low. Someone who scores low on attention will tend to have focus issues.

Davidson's studies concluded that our Emotional Style is largely based on the genes that we inherit from our ancestors, yet how we express each style is dependent on our environment—how we were raised. In Davidson's words, "genes load the gun, but only the environment can pull the trigger." To expand upon this analogy, a "violence gene" (the MAOA) has been identified. It has been determined that the expression of this gene—antisocial behavior—is far LESS likely to get expressed when someone with the gene is raised in a loving, caring environment. Conversely, if someone having the gene was abused, antisocial behavior is far MORE likely to be exhibited.

What does all this mean? Our brains have a property called *neuroplasticity*—our brain literally changes based on the thoughts and intentions that we bring to it. No matter what our Emotional Style is, we can change it, we can improve it, based on our intentional thoughts and actions.

Name It to Tame It

A sudden mood change (and we all have them) is almost always from an unfelt emotion that was latent in us for a period. Like a seed that lies beneath the soil, waiting for rain and sun, the right environment to grow. The unfelt emotion simply needs the right trigger to set it off, then poof! Out it comes, seemingly out of nowhere.

Suppressing emotions, trying not to feel them, doesn't work. This takes more energy and these emotions don't go away. They stay in the limbic system of our brain, fully aroused, waiting for something to trigger them into action.

"Anything exposed by the light becomes visible, for anything that becomes visible is light" (Eph 5:13). At every workshop, I ask people… "who in the last week has been angry? Sad? Felt guilt or regret? Lonely?" Almost everyone raises their hand at least once. Some raise their hands rather hesitantly for all. But this is good! And I do this for a reason. I want participants to name their emotions. When we name our emotions, when we put them into words—one or two is fine—we literally change our brain by sending calming signals from the "upstairs" brain to the "downstairs" brain. The next time you feel angry, say it! "I feel angry!" You don't act out your anger, you simply name it. When you do, you'll begin to throttle down your subcortical brain and activate your left cortex, where positive emotions are.

With any emotion, particularly ones that upset us, there are four A's to consider.

- **Accept** your emotion as it is. The emotion is there for a reason. Don't suppress or deny the way you feel.

- **Analyze** why you feel this way. Take a minute to process and determine the cause. There could be endless possibilities as to the source of why you feel how you feel. Try not to jump to a quick conclusion.

- **Act** on it. Allow yourself to experience the emotion for a short time, but then find healthy ways to express it and release it. Confide in a trusted friend. Journal.

- Make **Amends**. Seek or extend forgiveness (to be discussed further). Different emotions may require different forms or levels of forgiveness. Making amends might simply mean making things right with ourselves.

Anger

Before the beginning of a workshop, Sandy got a call from a woman who was trying to figure out a way to get her angry husband to attend. Sandy listened attentively to her concerns. Her husband had suffered through multiple losses and was quite distraught. The woman knew her husband could benefit from this workshop but convincing him was another story. Sandy told the woman that she had one job, to get her husband there the opening night and we would take it from there.

He came that first night. He is now known in our workshops as the "angry man." I never met him but saw him the first night pacing back and forth. I knew this had to be him. It was. I was skeptical whether he would come back the next week. He did. In fact, he came to all five sessions. By the end of the workshop, his wife told Sandy she noticed a difference in him. His anger had changed, maybe not for good, but for the better.

Anger is a powerful emotion associated with grief. It is a protest against an unpredictable world, where our desires are not being met. It's an emotion that focuses our thoughts in the past, about something that was done to us, or something that happened against our wishes. It's often a confusing emotion. Unless our loved one died from a completed suicide, anger at the deceased seems pointless. Why would I be angry at someone who didn't want to die? Yet often the source of our anger is at our loved one who left us alone, grieving and in a place we do not want to be.

Anger is first experienced in our body as emotion, and then expressed as a feeling with the thoughts we bring to it. The emotion of anger is meant to last just a few seconds. Feeling angry can last much longer, depending on what we do about it and how we use the four A's.

Emotions such as anger should cause us to approach the source of what made us angry in the first place. Letting anger simmer and turn inward, and onto ourselves, can lead to depression.

So, who are we angry at? God? Our loved one? The medical community? Our self? The anger we feel does more harm to ourself than to anyone towards whom we are angry. It raises cortisol (a stress hormone) levels, which in turn weakens our immunity, raises blood sugar levels and affects our sleep patterns.

Anger that is not adequately acknowledged, accepted and processed could complicate the mourning process. St. Paul tells us in Ephesians that it's okay to be angry but it's not okay to sin. In other words, it's okay to be angry, it's not okay to be an angry person. It's not okay to let this feeling take over and control your life. So, be angry, but do something positive with your anger. Try to cool down. Analyze why. Vent it. Walk it off. Punch a pillow. Direct your anger at its source. Forgive whomever made you angry. Try not to displace your anger onto others, who have nothing to do with why you are angry in the first place.

Venting

In small doses, venting can be helpful in releasing short-term tension. We feel better when we "blow off" some steam, right? Yet venting isn't action-oriented; it doesn't change the situation we are in. If venting only begets more venting, our negativity might increase and so could our anger. So if we need to vent, set a time limit of a few minutes. Then get back to finding solutions using the Four A's: Accept—Analyze—Act—Amend.

Communication

There is *passive* communication where someone else gets what they want but we don't. Then there is *aggressive* communication where only we get what we want. There is also *assertive* communication where both sides give and get some of what they want. If we are too passive, we get run over. If we are too aggressive we put the other person on the defense and push them away. Assertive communication seeks a win-win outcome, and approaches the other with compassion and understanding. Always seek first to understand, then to be understood.

Guilt and Regret

Like anger, guilt is a common emotional reaction with grief that's focus is in a past we are incapable of changing. Guilt is a feeling we have when we think we did something wrong, or violated some standard or personal code of conduct. By its very definition, guilt implies intent to harm. Yet we could also feel guilt over something we purposefully didn't do. It is a perception that our intentional behavior caused physical or emotional maltreatment to someone. It is our conscience. For example, we got into an argument the day before our loved one died in a car accident. We feel guilt and think we are responsible for this accident. We ruminate over this, which only adds to our guilt.

Regret is the "if only" or "I wish" emotion. What we did here was not intentional, but inadvertent. Nonetheless, we'd like to go back in time and change what we did or did not do. A lady at one of our workshops, whose husband died of a heart attack while shoveling snow, told me she regretted not helping him. She felt her unintentional omission of assistance was somehow the reason he died.

There are four main types of guilt that are associated with grief:

Cultural Guilt—It's not okay that we feel enough guilt over our son's suicide or drug overdose, but sometimes well-meaning friends and family add to our guilt and make us feel even worse. They may cause us to question our behavior. "Why didn't you see this coming?" "Could you have prevented this?"

Causal Guilt—With this type of guilt, we have or at least believe we have some culpability. A miscarriage would be an example of this. Called the "loneliest grief of all," the expectant mother feels something she did or did not do caused the baby to self-abort. Another example would be an accident where we were involved. Sandy tells the story of her mother's car accident that left her paralyzed. Her father was the driver and I'm sure for years felt tremendous guilt.

Moral Guilt—Moral guilt is when we believe that we violated a religious doctrine. Abortion might carry with it moral guilt. Not having a priest administer the sacrament of last rites before our loved one died could be another.

Survivor's Guilt—After someone dies, we may feel guilty that we survived, and they did not. Survivors guilt is often associated with post-traumatic stress and could pertain to, but is not limited to, veterans, 9/11 survivors, first responders, and transplant recipients.

At all our workshops we show a film clip from the movie, Ordinary People.[8] Conrad was the younger son. His brother was Buck. They were out boating when a storm came up. The boat flipped. Conrad hung on to the boat until help arrived, while Buck became too weak and drowned. Conrad was tormented with guilt, so much so, that he became depressed and made a failed attempt at suicide. He reluctantly began seeing a psychologist, Dr. Berger. After several sessions, they finally had a breakthrough. Conrad had convinced himself that he was somehow responsible for Buck's death. He kept telling himself, "I've got to get off the hook!" At the same time he was tired of beating himself up. His guilt had worn him down.

Dr. Berger adroitly put Conrad's guilt to a reality test and asked him. "What was the one wrong thing you did?" He waited while Conrad searched his mind for the answer.

"I hung onto the boat," replied Conrad.

"Exactly," replied Dr. Berger, "Now you can live with that, can't you?"

"I'm scared!" said Conrad.

"Feelings are scary," said Dr. Berger, "but if you can't feel pain, you won't feel anything else either."

Guilt or regret needs a "reality test." Ask yourself. What was the one wrong thing you did? Is it real or imagined? Would it have changed anything? When are you going to stop beating yourself up? Can you live with what you did or what you didn't do? What can you learn from this experience and do differently next time? Can you find purpose and meaning from this that will help others? Can you seek forgiveness? Can you forgive yourself? Have you asked for God's forgiveness through the sacrament of Reconciliation?

The past doesn't bend. Accept this fact. If guilt is weighing on you, use this as an impetus toward productive action. If your guilt is associated with your loved one, write them a letter, share your feelings, all of them. Any unresolved issues and hurt feelings from years ago that are still weighing on you now, get them out. All of them! Then burn the letter, or bury it or put it in a balloon and send it up in the air, releasing it. This will help you to begin to let go of your regretful actions from the past that you cannot change now. It may help you to let go of any guilty feelings that you have from the past that you cannot now change.

Depression | Complicated Grief | Healthy Grief

Depression can be used broadly to define the benign blues that we all experience from time to time. Major Depression on the other hand is a chronic mental illness, and is quite malignant. Today we see epidemic levels of this illness, ten times higher than it was in 1960. The mean onset age has been cut in half and is now only fifteen years of age. More women become depressed, or at least seek treatment, but more men act it out in the form of suicide attempts or other self-destructive behaviors.

Abraham Lincoln said of his depression, "I am now the most miserable man living." Major Depression is a profound disorder of both the mind and the body. Only a trained therapist can diagnose someone with MD vis-à-vis normal healthy grief. It is treatable with medication, behavior changes, such as exercise, and cognitive behavioral therapy, but is often an enduring condition.

Because depressives fear feeling, "feelings are scary," they get very good at being depressed. They work harder at living, but very little joy comes from these efforts. The opposite of depression isn't happiness, but vitality—the ability to experience a full range of emotions: good and bad, happiness and sadness. To not feel negative emotions, depressives tend to shut down *all* emotions. It's like the old Christmas lights. When one light went out, the whole string went dark.

> Love and loss comes in a single package. Psychological vitality and openness to hurt are two sides of the same coin. If you are unable to risk loss, you are un-

able to live a vital life. If you are unwilling to be hurt, you are unable to love.[9]

Freud believed that with grief the world feels empty, but with depression, the person feels empty, lost and hopeless. Only about one-third of all people with depression will seek professional care and treatment. And of course, without treatment, depression slowly wears out the human body.

There is this story of an experiment done with a walleyed pike and the minnows in a fish tank. At first, minnows are dropped into the tank and the pike happily eats them all. Then a glass partition was placed in between the pike and the minnows. The pike rams his snout against the glass repeatedly but is denied the delicacy of the minnows. After a day or two he gives up trying. He looks but does not charge the glass. Then the glass is removed. The pike again has full access to the minnows. Yum! But no. At this point the pike has lost hope in ever having another minnow for lunch. He only looks at the minnows and dares not eat a one of them. He dies from starvation.

Someone who is depressed sees life going on all around them, but they find it difficult to join in. They try repeatedly, just as the pike did, but then they slowly give up hope that they will ever get to the other side where all the goodness is.

Though they have similar characteristics, grief and Major Depression (MD) are not the same. Grief is not an illness, it's an automatic reaction to loss where the intensity will often attenuate over time. The grief process is assisted by the intentional ways in which we mourn and learn to adapt to this loss.

Complicated Grief (CG), or another term, Persistent Complex Bereavement Disorder (PCBD), occurs in about 7-10% of all grieving people and is considered a severe form of grief. This disorder is now recognized by DSM-5 (*Diagnostic and Statistical Manual for Mental Disorders*) as something different than Major Depression (MD). The DSM-5 asserts that grief does not preclude someone from having MD, and that MD can be heightened and/or triggered by grief. Complicated Grief according to Dr. Katherine Shear, the program director at Columbia University Center for Complicated Grief, occurs when "something interferes with the process of healing, blocking acceptance and adaptation to the loss."[10] This results in the grieving person feeling "stuck" in acute grief.

Grief or Major Depression

There are differences between grief and Major Depression. According to Dr. Sidney Zisook, Director of Psychiatry at the University of California, these differences manifest in several ways.[11]

With grief, the state of unease (dysphoria), tends to decrease in the weeks and months that follow. *Grief can feel like a rollercoaster.* Waves of grief may occur with thoughts and reminders of the deceased, but they are not constant. *Depression feels like a dead end.* With MD, this unease tends to be more persistent and not tied to specific memories or thoughts of the lost loved one.

Someone who is grieving in a healthy way may have both positive and negative emotions where laughter and tears are a part of everyday life. They experience vitality—joy and sadness. But with MD, the unhappy mood is more pervasive, leaving little or no room for joy.

Grieving people tend to find comfort in being consoled. Someone in MD finds little comfort in this support and tends to be more isolated and withdrawn.

With grief, thoughts and memories of the deceased are normal and healthy. With MD, these thoughts tend to focus on the depressed individual being unworthy or even bad.

Perhaps one of principal differences between grief and depression is self-esteem. Self-esteem is generally preserved in healthy grief. The grieving person feels bad about what happened, but not bad about themselves. With someone in a Major Depressive Episode, thoughts of hopelessness and self-loathing are far more common, as are suicidal ideations.

A trained therapist will examine three key markers to make a diagnosis of Major Depression or Complicated Grief.

1. Severity of the symptoms.

2. Duration of the symptoms.

3. Pathology or impairment of daily function.

This book does not have the scope to cover Major Depression or Complicated Grief in the broad detail it deserves. Anyone who thinks that they have Major Depression or Complicated Grief should seek additional help and counseling. For immediate help, call 9-1-1.

Forgiveness

In 2016, I listened to the best homily I've ever heard. It was from a visiting priest, and was about forgiveness. He said that in order to understand forgiveness, we must first understand the cross. The homily went something like this:

> You and I have been good friends for years. We just had dinner together at your house. After dinner we get into an argument, you name the subject. In my fit of anger, I look down and see your priceless pocket watch that your grandfather gave you years ago sitting undisturbed on your coffee table. You cherish this watch. You protect it and only had it out because you wanted to take it to your trusted jeweler to have it cleaned and repaired. In my rage, I grab the watch and throw it to the floor. I then proceed to stomp on it, breaking it into many pieces, destroying the watch beyond repair. I then run out the front door.
>
> A week later I call you and ask if I can come over. You pause for a moment, remembering all too well my outburst and the destroyed pocket watch. But you decide to take the high road and welcome me back into your home. Upon arrival I am remorseful and apologize for what I did. I cannot repay you. I cannot repair what I broke. But I ask for your forgiveness anyway. And you, following the lead of Christ, forgive me for what I did. By forgiving me of my transgression, you took on a debt I could not repay.

What does this teach us about forgiveness? Christ took on all our debt, all our sins, that we could not possibly repay, and he nailed them to the cross. His cross. He paid the price for our salvation by washing away our transgressions. In this example, you paid the price for my sin. You forgave me. And in forgiving me, you canceled my debt which I could not repay. You wiped it clean. This is what Christ did for all of us. This is what we must do for others. We cannot call ourselves Christian if we do not forgive others and seek forgiveness from others. "Like oil, forgiveness neutralizes friction" (Fr. Raniero Cantalamessa, the Pontifical Household Preacher).[12]

Forgiveness is not an emotion, it's a choice. Often a difficult choice, yet if we are to be faith-filled Christians, it's a necessary choice. "Forgive us our trespasses, *as we forgive those who trespass against us.*" What's Jesus telling us here? He wants us to learn how to forgive as He forgives. If we can't forgive others as He forgives us time and time again, should we even pray the Lord's Prayer?

Forgiveness is letting go of the right for personal payback. We put down the rock. We look in the mirror and recognize ourselves as sinners; though striving to be better, we are far from unblemished, far from perfect. To be sure, if we put the person who wronged us in the same mirror, we would also see a flawed human, like us, striving to be better, failing all the time. Yet we forgive anyway, and in relinquishing any personal payback, we surrender any power that they have over us.

If forgiveness neutralizes friction, unforgiveness forces a slow and steady leak of the lubricant we need to forgive—which is love. Without the neutralizing agent of love, we give power to bitterness and resentment. We give power to the very things that corrode the engine of a once fruitful relationship, bringing it to sudden halt.

I remember as growing up my mother would caution me not to run with scissors in my hand. What was she afraid of? The scissors by themselves were not dangerous. But I wasn't thinking of the harm they could cause if I fell on them. She was in essence, protecting me from myself.

When we choose not to forgive, we are running too—away from love, away from God, and towards the source of our pain. Running away from love and God is only part of the problem, because with unforgiveness we run with a two-edged sword in our hand. One side is the anger we feel; the other side is our own desire to be right, rather than to do the right thing. When we slip and fall, the sword cuts closest to the one holding it.

God forgives, because God is love. "For I will forgive their inequities and remember their sins no more" (Jer 31:34). At the same time, if we choose to hold onto our grudges and resentments of others, if we choose not to forgive, God will not forgive us either. "For if you forgive men their trespasses, your heavenly father will forgive you; but if you do not forgive men their trespasses, neither will your father forgive your trespasses" (Matt 6:14-15). The choice is always ours.

The Buddhists have a saying; "It is not with resentment that resentment is placated; it is with non-resentment that resentment is mitigated." Nelson Mandela teaches, "Resentment is like drinking poison and hoping it will kill your enemies." Nelson Mandela also said that as he left prison, if he didn't leave his anger, hatred and bitterness behind, he'd still be in prison. Shine a light into any darkness and the darkness vanishes. Shine love into any bitterness or hatred, and the bitterness or hatred vanishes. They cannot coexist. Light or darkness. Love or hate.

To be clear, forgiveness doesn't condone what happened! It doesn't change what happened either. It doesn't change the source of our anger or resentment. We can't un-ring the bell. But we don't have to keep ringing it either, over and over, letting our mind chew on what happened. Forgiveness doesn't negate any need for justice.

> Forgiving is hard work. It takes time and involves pain. It's not just a simple declaration or automatic, reflexive action. False forgiveness is going through the motions without anything changing on the inside. It's lip service, and it actually interferes with the authentic resolution and estranges people from their real feelings.[13]

But with true forgiveness, we stop the cycle of rumination. We change our emotional response to the person who harmed us and the way in which we were harmed. We choose to take back control. We choose love over hate. We choose the future over the past.

> Remembering grievances works great damage. It is accompanied by anger, fosters sin and brings a hatred for justice. It is a rusty arrow spreading poison in the soul. Be lovers of peace, the most precious treasure that anyone can desire.[14]

Perhaps this point is best illustrated with St. Peter. During the transfiguration on the mountain, Peter tells Jesus he wants to build three "booths." Peter is obtuse in his understanding that the mountain would not hold Jesus, that the Lord's mission is well beyond earth. In the Garden of Gethsemane, Peter falls asleep three times. During the Passion, he denies knowing Jesus three times, one of those times warming himself beside a charcoal fire.

How must Peter feel? Time and again he lets his Lord down. He acts thick-headed, unprepared, and cowardly. So much so that Jesus calls the man Satan! Does it get any worse than that? Does Peter secretly hope that he'll never have to face his Lord again? Does he secretly hope he can go back and be a simple fisherman and end all this "pick up your cross and follow me" stuff? Does Peter really believe that Christ will die and then rise again as He predicted He would?

Isn't Peter like all of us? Deeply flawed. Doubting. Scared. Running from our troubles. Wouldn't it be nice to know what was running through Peter's brain that Easter Sunday night? The doors were closed and in walks the Man, wounds and all, the very man Peter walked away from. What does Jesus do? He smiles and makes eye contact. The disciples were glad to see Jesus. Was Peter? "Peace be with you," He says. He breathes on them, giving them the Holy Spirit. "If you forgive the sins of any, they are forgiven; if you retain the sins of any, they are retained."

Peter must be thinking, wait a minute. You offer us peace. You give us the gift of the Holy Spirit. You talk forgiveness. You mean you're not angry at us?

But seeing isn't believing for Peter. He still doesn't get it. He doesn't yet understand that despite his flaws, and notwithstanding his human inadequacies, he's about to receive a big promotion. So, a few days later, Peter escapes one last time to the Sea of Tiberias to return to what he's known most of his life, fishing. His friends go with him. But this poor band of fishermen can't catch a darn thing until Jesus comes along, the third time in His resurrected form, and tells them where the fish are.

Now, with the net full of fish, Peter is the first to swim to shore. He finally gets it. Jesus is there waiting for him. He's built a charcoal fire, to grill the fish, but perhaps also to bring Peter back too, remember that time you were warming yourself by the fire while I was being tortured?

And then the talk begins.

"Simon, son of John, do you love me more than these?"

"Yes Lord, you know that I love you."

"Feed my lambs."

"Simon, son of John, do you love me?

"Yes Lord, you know I love you."

"Tend to my sheep."

"Do you love me?"

"Lord, you know everything, you know that I love you."

"Feed my sheep."

Three unnecessary booths. Three times falling asleep in the garden. Three times denying he knows Jesus. But Jesus doesn't rummage through Peter's past, filled with mistakes and failures, hoping to make Peter feel worse. Three times, Jesus offers Peter the opportunity to express his love for his Lord. Then, all is forgiven. All is well. Here are the keys to my Kingdom. "On this rock, I will build my church."

Forgiveness is a two-way street. We seek forgiveness to release our own guilt about what we did or didn't do. We extend forgiveness to release the bitterness and resentment that we are carrying around about something done to us. Too many of us hold open old wounds, some we inflicted upon others, some we own as the consequence of our actions. Forgiveness closes these wounds, so they can finally heal.

Forgiveness and reconciliation are not synonymous. Forgiveness is between us and God. Reconciliation is between two people. Forgiveness is needed for there to be reconciliation, but forgiveness does not always lead to reconciliation. We can choose to forgive, but for various reasons not reconcile the relationship or even seek justice.

The *Catechism of the Catholic Church* teaches about forgiveness:

> Christian prayer extends to the forgiveness of enemies, transfiguring the disciple by configuring him to his Master. Forgiveness is the high-point of Christian prayer; only hearts attuned to God's compassion can receive the gift of prayer. Forgiveness also bears witness that, in our world, love is stronger than sin. The martyrs of yesterday and today bear this witness to Jesus. Forgiveness is the fundamental condition of the reconciliation of children of God with the Father and of men with one another (CCC §2844).

Whom do we need to forgive? Why is it sometimes that the person we most need to forgive is the person we live with 24 hours a day, seven days a week, 365 days a year? God wants to forgive us, all of us. In fact, He's quite good at it. We just need to open the door to our heart and ask. And the best time to ask is the present time, because that's all there is. The past is water downstream. It's gone. The future is water upstream. But the water is only here for us at this precise moment in time called the present. This is always the best time because it's always the only time. Try to forgive now and always.

Gratefulness

The antithesis of gratitude is resentment. Like forgiveness, resentment is a choice. We become resentful when we choose not to forgive. When we choose to forgive, we let go the resentment luggage that we have carried with us every hour of every day, weighing us down, exhausting us. Being resentful and unforgiving holds us back from being imitators of Christ and from seizing upon every moment as a gift. It's as if we are the prodigal son or daughter, and on our return home, we run past the outstretched arms of our father, who has waited ever so patiently for our embrace.

> Gratitude as a discipline involves a conscious choice. I can choose to be grateful even when my emotions and feelings are steeped in hurt and resentment. It's amazing how many occasions present themselves in which I can choose gratitude instead of complaint.[15]

Gratitude is a choice. It requires appreciation for the many gifts we have been given. Simply searching for these gifts has a positive impact on our brain's chemistry. The search alone releases serotonin and dopamine—both neurotransmitters—that help to regulate different regions of our brain, including love, joy, mood and motivation. Increased amounts of these neurotransmitters help to neutralize the effects of anxiety and depression.

Like any new behavior, gratitude takes practice. Buy a pack of post-it notes. For one week, each morning, write one thing for which you are grateful. It might simply be that the sun is out today. I heard birds chirping. I have a warm house to live in. Post these notes on a wall in your house where you will see them a few times each day. These notes will be reminders of the things you are grateful for. Even if things all around you might seem to be falling, this one wall might help to hold you up.

Summary

Pain is a part of being human. Fr. Richard Rohr wrote, "All great spirituality is about what we do with our pain."[16] We all experience pain, either physical, emotional or both. Pain is a signal that something is wrong, and we must try to do something to make it right. When we yield to this pain, we face it, we don't run from it. Our emotions are designed to help us approach or avoid the source which is triggering our emotion. Emotions that are not properly defused can lead to more serious concerns such as depression. Forgiveness is a process, but we must always forgive as Christ always forgives us.

PERSONAL

Questions to reflect on:

What emotions are you dealing with now?

Whom do you need to forgive?

Write one thing for which you are grateful.

Works of Mercy: Forgive Offenses

Make amends with someone you have hurt or someone who has hurt you. Commit to going to Confession in the next thirty days and then try to go at least three to four times each year.

Take some quiet time to write...

Your Fourth Intention:
Yield to the Pain

It is my intention to...

NOTES

1. PBS, "From Jesus to Christ: The First Christians," *Frontline* (Season 16, Episode 10). 6 April 1998.

2. Fr. James Martin, "What Does It Mean to Carry Our Cross?" *Northwest Catholic*. (Diocese of Seattle, 12 November 2014).

3. St. Pope John Paul II, *Salvifici Doloris* (*On the Christian Meaning of Suffering*). 11 February 1984, §7.

4. Antonio Damasio, "The Importance of Feelings: Understanding the Difference Between Emotions and Feelings," *WakeupWorld.com*. 24 April 2015.

5. Antonio Damasio, *Looking for Spinoza*. Harcourt, 2004.

6. Rebecca Kowalski, *Sandy Hook Five Years Later*. 2017.

7. Richard J. Davidson Ph.D., *The Emotional Life of Your Brain*. (New York, Plume, 2013).

8. *Ordinary People*, Film, (Paramount Pictures, 1980).

9. Steven C. Hayes, Ph.D., "From Loss to Love," *Psychology Today*, July 2018. https://www.psychologytoday.com/us/articles/201806/loss-love, accessed 26 October 2018.

10. Dr. Katherine Shear and Dr. Sidney Zisook, "Complicated Grief Treatment Trumps Depression Therapy," *Medscape*, 25 September 2014.

11. Ibid.

12. Fr. Raniero Cantalamessa, Why Forgive? Homily, 9 September 2005. https://zenit.org/articles/why-forgive-father-cantalamessa-responds/, accessed 26 October 2018.

13. Jeanne Safer, "Must You Forgive?" Psychology Today, 1 July 1999. https://www.psychologytoday.com/us/articles/199907/must-you-forgive, accessed 26 October 2018.

14. St. Francis Paola, "Turn To the Lord With a Pure Heart" Letter, AD 1486, Vatican Archives, http://www.vatican.va/spirit/documents/spirit_20010402_francesco-paola_en.html, accessed 26 October 2018.

15. Henri J. M. Nouwen, *The Return of the Prodigal Son*. (Doubleday, 1994).

16. Richard Rohr, *What the Mystics Know*. (The Crossroad Publishing Company, 2015).from being imitators of Christ and from seizing upon every moment as a gift. It's as if we are the prodigal son or daughter, and on our return home, we run past the outstretched arms of our father, who has waited ever so patiently for our embrace.

 POPE BENEDICT XVI

Only when the future is certain as a positive reality does it become possible to live the present well.

CHAPTER 7

The Fifth Intention:
Enduring Connection

PRAYERFUL

Beloved, do not be surprised at the fiery ordeal which comes upon you to prove you, as though something strange were happening to you. But rejoice in so far as you share in Christ's sufferings, that you may also rejoice and be glad when His glory is revealed. (1 PET 4:12-13)

Let us pray. *In the name of the Father, and of the Son and the Holy Spirit.*

Soul of Jesus, sanctify me. Blood of Jesus, wash me. Passion of Jesus, comfort me. Wounds of Jesus, hide me. Heart of Jesus, receive me. Spirit of Jesus, enliven me. Beauty of Jesus, draw me. Humility of Jesus, humble me. Peace of Jesus, pacify me. Love of Jesus, inflame me. Kingdom of Jesus, come to me. Grace of Jesus, replenish me. Mercy of Jesus, pity me. Purity of Jesus, purify me. Cross of Jesus, support me. Nails of Jesus, hold me. Mouth of Jesus, bless me.

Elizabeth Ann Seton, pray for us.

For it will be as when a man going on a journey called his servants and entrusted to them his property; to one he gave five talents, to another two, to another one, to each according to his ability. Then he went away. He who had received the five talents went at once and traded with them; and he made five talents more. So also, he who had the two talents made two talents more. But he who had received the one talent went and dug in the ground and hid his master's money.

Now after a long time the master of those servants came and settled accounts with them. And he who had received the five talents came forward, bringing five talents more, saying, "Master, you delivered to me five talents; here I have made five talents more." His master said to him, "Well done, good and faithful servant; you have been faithful over a little, I will set you over much; enter into the joy of your master." And he also who had the two talents came forward, saying, "Master, you delivered to me two talents; here I have made two talents more." His master said to him, "Well done, good and faithful servant; you have been faithful over a little, I will set you over much; enter into the joy of your master."

He also who had received the one talent came forward, saying, "Master, I knew you to be a hard man, reaping where you did not sow, and gathering where you did not winnow; so I was afraid, and I went and hid your talent in the ground. Here you have what is yours." But his master answered him, "You wicked and slothful servant! You knew that I reap where I have not sowed, and gather where I have not winnowed? Then you ought to have invested my money with the bankers, and at my coming I should have received what was my own with interest. So, take the talent from him, and give it to him who has the ten talents. For to everyone who has will more be given, and he will have abundance; but from him who has not, even what he has will be taken away. And cast the worthless servant into the outer darkness; there men will weep and gnash their teeth." (Matt 25:14-30)

PRACTICAL

W hat does it mean to have an enduring connection with someone we love who has died? How do we have a relationship with someone who is no longer physically with us? We can't talk with them the way we used to. The way we'd look at their face when they would speak. Language is a gateway into our minds, a complex system of neural pathways. So, their words would reverberate into our ears and then our minds would interpret what was said and form meaning to it. We would respond. A conversation would ensue. This was life as we knew it. That was then.

But this is now.

What is prayer if it is not a conversation with the invisible God? We pray to God the Father, through Jesus, because we want to open our heart and let Him in. Let Him see how broken we are (even if He knows). We pour out our petitions to Him, praise Him, and tell Him the times we have fallen short (even if He knows). So, what is prayer, if it is not a form of communication or dialogue with our Father in heaven? A communication that looks outward. "not to the things that are seen, but to the things that are unseen" (2 Cor 4:18). We encounter Him through our faith and our prayer life. The Reverend Billy Graham was once asked "is God dead?" To which he replied, "No." Pressed again, he was asked, "how do know for sure?" The Reverend simply said with most assurance, "I spoke with him this morning."

The now famous line from Morrie Schwartz (*Tuesdays with Morrie*, by Mitch Albom) is so true, "Death ends a life, not a relationship."[1] The bonds of love endure the permanence of death. The relationship though permanently changed, can be reconstructed in beautiful and meaningful ways. A process that is both intentional and personal, and offers the opportunity for new life, through a new expression of love. "Though it feels like despair, mourning has a deeper and more authentic name: hope. Jesus praises sorrow, the virtue of continuing to love in the midst of ruinous circumstances, which is the opposite of resignation to irretrievable loss. Unlike stoic resignation, hopeful mourning is a Christian virtue.[2]

The Quest for Meaning

Viktor Frankl wrote that "The quest for meaning was essential to mental health and human flourishing."[3] When we have something to live for, we find the means to live. It is hard to let go of the past when our future looks bleak, but our quest for meaning and purpose gives us the opportunity to paint a different picture of what tomorrow can look like. Frankl said suffering minus meaning equals despair. Well then, suffering plus meaning must equal hope.

Several studies demonstrate that 50-80% of parents who lose a child through an accident, homicide or suicide will seek to find meaning and purpose in their loss. These parents grieved their loss, then became intentional about mourning their loss. They looked beyond themselves and toward a cause. They intend to create a future that is better for others, while honoring their own past that was filled with love and joy.

> A fundamental proposition of constructivism is that humans are motivated to construct and maintain a meaningful self-narrative, defined as an overarching cognitive-affective behavioral structure that organizes the micro-narratives of everyday life into a micro-narrative that consolidates our self-understanding, establishes our character range of emotions and goals, and guides our performance on the stage of the social world. (ROBERT NEIMEYER)[4]

Our sense of who we are, our identity, is very much contained within a self-narrative of the stories that we share with others. Our life and our stories, much like a novel, have an arc to them. Though all stories, all lives, are not the same, there is predictability, a pattern of similarities to many stories within them. Birth-growth-education-career-love-marriage-children-grand-children-death. Of course, there are detours that break off from the main narrative, such as divorce, illness, money issues, career change, death of a loved one. These may seem at the time like departures from the main narrative, the bucolic life we intended to have, where trouble stayed outside our white picket fence. It is then our responsibility to assimilate our suffering paths, our detours in life, back into the broader arc of our self-narrative, not collapsing under the weight of our cross, but taking it up, holding it high and finding meaning in it.

> **ENDURING CONNECTION**
>
> An enduring connection extends the bonds forged in life that have been cut short by death and attempts to reconstruct the relationship in a personal and meaningful way. It is different than an event or ceremony, that looks inward, it is a mission of redemptive healing that looks outward.

> To live is to suffer; to survive is to find meaning in the suffering—if there is a purpose in life at all, there must be a purpose in suffering and dying—but no-one can tell another what that purpose is.[5]

Viktor Frankl said that we find meaning in our lives from purposeful work, love and the courage to face difficulties. His concept of meaning is not discovered in the "why" something happens to us, but rather in our response to the "why." Friedrich Nietzsche's quote "He who has a why to live for can bear almost any how," is relevant here. If we have a higher purpose in our life, we can bear almost any burden that comes our way. We don't find meaning in how our wife got cancer, or how our son felt his only alternative was to end his life. These questions can tear us apart, thread by thread, until we completely unravel in despair. Meaning is not likely to be found in the innumerable questions of our suffering, it is discovered in the acceptance of it, our attitude towards it, the actions we take because of it and a new calling, a new purpose, a new personal growth we find in it. A loved one's death, once accepted, can lead us to our own existential questions; why am I alive? What is my purpose? How can

I make a difference?

Frankl believed that we always have the power to choose our attitude in any given set of circumstances—to choose our own way. And it is in choosing our response that we find meaning. Every hour of every day we have opportunities to either protect or renounce our freedom to choose our attitude.

Redemptive Suffering

As humans we search for meaningful answers as to why we suffer. This can often be a misguided mission, leading us to see only what is gone, "for the things that are seen are transient, but the things that are unseen are eternal" (2 COR 4:18).

> Pain is part of being human. Anyone who really wanted to get rid of suffering would have to get rid of love before anything else, because there can be no love without suffering, because it always demands an element of self-sacrifice, because, given temperamental differences and drama of situations, it will always bring with it renunciation and pain. Anyone who has inwardly accepted suffering becomes more mature and more understanding of others, becomes more human. Anyone who consistently avoids suffering does not understand other people, he becomes harsh and selfish. If we say that suffering is the inner side of love, we then understand why it is so important to learn how to suffer.[6]

Salvation was not given to us when Christ walked on water or turned water into wine or when he healed the leper. We were saved through one thing. Suffering. His suffering. Suffering is derived from the words *sacrum facere*, which means to make sacred, to make holy. The saints are holy in The Church Triumphant because they gave of themselves to others. Mary gave of herself to birth the Son of God. Maximilian Kolbe gave his life, so that a father and husband could live. "The only real sadness, the only real failure, the only great tragedy in life, is not to become a saint."[7] Christ, in his own suffering on the cross, showed that seemingly in His moment of great weakness, there was power. Christ's ministry was never more energized, than when He was immobilized on a cross. "My grace is sufficient for you, for my power is made perfect in weakness" (2 Cor 12:9).

However. the cross is not symbolic; it was used by God to redeem mankind. St. Paul wrote in his letter to the Colossians, "Now I rejoice in my sufferings for your sake, and in my flesh, I complete what is lacking in Christ afflictions for the sake of the body, that is, the Church. Christ's Redemptive Mission, His suffering on the cross for our sake, was in no way lacking or defective. It completed our salvation. This is what the Church recognizes as Objective Redemption. By His cross, suffering, death and resurrection, He "paid the price" for our reconciliation with the Father. "He gave His life for the ransom of many" (Matt 20:28).

Shortly before Christ died He said, "It is finished." But it was in a very real sense only the beginning of the story, not the end. Because we, as the Body of Christ, on a never-ending Lenten quest, must be sharers in His Redemptive mission, His suffering. Our suffering endured without Christ can be meaningless, but with Christ can be meaningful. "Whoever looks for Jesus without the cross, will find the cross without Jesus, that is, he will certainly find the cross, but not the strength to carry it."[8]

In suffering for our salvation, Christ transformed human suffering and elevated it to a supernatural level. Something greater than any miracle He performed. He gave us all the power, in the light of faith, to participate in God's plan of redemption. In doing so, we wed our wounds to His Son's. We magnify our pain, through prayer and voluntary penances, so that we can fill up what is lacking in His Church. Doing so, we become sharers in the redemptive sufferings of Christ. This is what the Church refers to as *Subjective Redemption*.

> Human suffering itself has been redeemed. The Redeemer suffered in place of man and for man. Every man has his own share in that suffering which the redemption has accomplished. He is called to share in that suffering through which all human suffering has also been redeemed. In bringing about the Redemption through suffering, Christ raised human suffering to the level of the Redemption. Thus, each man (and woman), in his (her) sufferings, can also become a sharer in the redemptive sufferings of Christ.[9]

In the previous chapter we learned from St. Pope John Paul II that "Man suffers when he experiences any kind of evil." Evil he defined as lack, limitation or distortion of good. Suffering is active in our lives when we are deprived or cut off from good. Love is good. Our love for the person for whom we grieve remains unbroken, but the relationship is now fragmented. There are limits and boundaries that weren't there before. We feel cut off from the good, so we suffer.

Christ's earthly ministry cared for those who suffered. He was the Good Samaritan and the Good Shepherd, reaching outward, past Himself, towards others in need, the poor, the infirm, the lost, the afflicted, the blind, and the castaways of society. When we stop alongside and avail ourselves and become sensitive to a suffering person, a grieving person, we become the Good Samaritan. A Good Samaritan, whether on the road from Jerusalem to Jericho or the road from grief to mourning, consoles, and brings assistance and hope to those who grieve, to those who suffer. "Redemptive suffering always generates immense life in others."[10]

> A true revolution of values will soon cause us to question the fairness and justice of many of our past and present policies. On the one hand, we are called to play the Good Samaritan on life's roadside, but that will be only an initial act. One day we must come to see that the whole Jericho Road must be transformed so that men and women will not be constantly beaten and robbed as they make their journey on life's highway. True compassion is more than flinging a coin to a beggar. It comes to see that an edifice which produces beggars needs restructuring.[11]

Each Lenten season we are asked to enter our own desert, draw closer to Christ and emerge at Easter more like Him. To be the face of Christ to others, we are called, even during our own suffering and grief, to reach outward, beyond ourselves, towards others in their suffering and grief. The Good Samaritan doesn't ask, "if I stop to help this person, what will happen to me?" The Good Samaritan asks, "if I don't stop what will happen to this person who needs my help?" The Good Samaritan answers the question, "who is my neighbor?"

The priest and Levite were bystanders on the road to Jericho. But we are not bystanders of Christ's Redemptive mission. We are recipients of His grace, and participants who must share in the redemptive suffering of Christ. "Beloved, do not be surprised at the fiery ordeal which comes upon you to prove you, as though something strange was happening to you. But rejoice in so far as you share in Christ's sufferings, that you may also rejoice and be glad when His glory is revealed" (1 PET 4:12-13).

Redemptive Mourning

The crucifixion of Jesus Christ was evil. An innocent and unblemished man, even if it was by His own choosing, was tortured, beaten and murdered. We celebrate His death every "Good" Friday; from the suffering Christ came a transformed good, our salvation, our liberation from ultimate evil, an eternal separation from God. "For God so loved the world that he gave his only begotten Son, that whoever believes in Him should not perish, but have eternal life" (JOHN 3:16).

> God does not give his joy to us for ourselves alone, and if we do possess him for ourselves alone we would not possess him at all. Any joy that does not overflow from our souls and help other people to rejoice in God does not come to us from God. But do not think that you have to see how it overflows into the souls of others. In the economy of grace, you may be sharing his gifts with someone you will never know until you get to heaven.[12]

In the garden, Adam was like the rest of us. He chose pleasure before suffering. Don't we all have a penchant for absorbing pleasure like a sponge and pain like a sieve? But Christ reversed this, "in exchange for the joy that was placed before Him, He submitted to the cross," (HEB 12:2). His suffering preceded pleasure, redemption, salvation. The suffering on the cross that Christ endured for you and I was evil, but His resurrection became the fruit of this evil. The fruit of the cross was the resurrection. His pain and suffering preceded our fruit. Christ changed the rules so that *salvation* is the last word, not death.

Christ's love for us is so deep and perfect, He offered himself in complete sacrifice unto death. Redemptive Suffering is aligned with this same sacrifice and this same love. We profit from the fruit of His sacrifice, to sacrifice our profits so they bear fruit in His kingdom.

With Redemptive Suffering we place our wounded body in His wounded body—"by his wounds we are healed" (Is 53:5)—for the sole purpose of letting God use our suffering, broadly defined and called forth by evil, for the good of others, for the good of His Church.

It is here that we pose a new thought; a subset of Redemptive Suffering called Redemptive Mourning. This is not to conflict with Church doctrine. Redemptive Mourning merely adheres to Redemptive Suffering, but forms a different, more specific bond of bereavement. As the resurrection followed suffering, so does mourning follow grief. Redemptive Mourning is our intentional cooperation, an act of love, where we identify our transformed wounds from mourning with the Risen Glorified Christ. We then let God's Grace, His supernatural power, bring meaning to our suffering, so that the fruit of our pain that we felt in grief, becomes the good news we bring to others in His Church. Pope Benedict says:

> Blessed are those who mourn, for they will be comforted" (MATT 5:4). Is it good to mourn, to declare oneself blessed? There are two kinds of mourning. The first is the kind that has lost hope, that has become mistrustful of love and of truth and that therefore eats away and destroys man from within. But there is also the mourning occasioned by the shattering encounter with the truth, which leads man to undergo conversion and to resist evil. This mourning heals, because it teaches man to hope and love again. Judas is an example of the first kind of mourning: Struck with horror of his own fall, he no longer dares to hope and hangs himself in despair. Peter is an example of the second kind: Struck by the Lord's gaze, he bursts into healing tears that plow up from the soil of his soul. He begins anew and is himself renewed.[13]

We humbly submit then, that Peter is a model for Redemptive Mourning. His tears and his grief led him to hope and renewal. As it should be with all Redemptive Mourners, the healing tears that form around our grief, one day will lead us back to a place of hope and to our own renewal in which we make it our mission to renew the lives of others.

Jesus Christ accepted His mission. He was very deliberate with everything He did, up to and including His death on a tree. You and I on the other hand, don't always know what we're doing. But even when we can't always make sense from the senseless, we always can make mission from the madness. Fr. John J. Hardon remarked that Pope John Paul's message on suffering was always the same… "Be patient and endure the cross of Christ, but at the same time seek to find ways of relieving human suffering caused by hatred, injustice and greed."[14] We can find some small way to make an impression on someone else. To be kind and caring. To be a disciple of hope to the hopeless. To be that Good Samaritan to someone who thought all goodness was gone from this world.

> Therefore, uniting myself with all of you who are suffering throughout the land of Poland, in your homes, in the hospitals, the clinics, the dispensaries, the sanatoria—wherever you may be—I beg you to make use *of the cross* that has become part of each one of you *for salvation*. I pray for you to have light and spiritual strength in your suffering, that you may not lose courage but may discover for yourselves the meaning of suffering and may be able to relieve others by prayer and sacrifice. And do not forget me and the whole of the Church, and the cause of the Gospel and peace that I am serving by Christ's will. You who are weak and humanly incapable, be a source of strength for your brother and father who is at your side in prayer and heart.[15]

Because Christ raised Redemptive Suffering to a supernatural level, He calls each of us to share our own suffering and grief, with His suffering and grief. In doing so, we are fully cooperating with the God of mercy, who will not let our sufferings be meaningless, but He will raise it to a meaningful level and use our suffering to work for the greater good in the body of Christ.

> I will rather boast most gladly of my weakness, in order that the power of Christ may dwell in me. Therefore, I am content with weaknesses, insults, hardships, persecutions and constraints, for the sake of Christ; for when I am weak, then I am strong (2 COR 12:8-10).

Whoever boasts of weaknesses or hardships? But it is exactly what St. Paul is asking us to do. To humble ourselves, to accept our trials and to trust and be open to what God might do with them. Isn't St. Paul telling us here that God is attracted to our weakness, for it is there that His power can dwell in us.

Prayer is one way we are connected with our loved ones. In fact, it should be one of our vocations in life to pray our loved ones home. And once home, they are saints, and can intercede on our and others' behalf. That's a good thing!

Here are some examples of stories that we have come across—of people, who after grieving the death of a loved one, decided to take powerful action as a way to honor the life of their loved one. They found meaning in death by their new-found mission in life. We believe these are powerful examples of Redemptive Mourners.

B.R.A.D. 21

When our daughter Morgan turned twenty-one, she was a student at Michigan State University. That February, shortly before her birthday, Morgan received a letter from the B.R.A.D. 21 (Be Responsible About Drinking) organization, a Michigan non-profit organization.

Bradley J. McCue had been a Michigan State junior when he turned twenty-one. The next day he died from alcohol poisoning. Brad's mother, Cindy McCue, began this organization in 1999 and it has since mailed out over 400,000 birthday cards to young students about to turn twenty-one. The card reads:

> It is our hope that the educational information distributed by this organization will prevent other families from suffering the loss we have experienced. We want you to turn 22… celebrate responsibly.

Brad's parents and friends were deeply impacted by the loss of their son and friend. But their response to Brad's death has been remarkable. Their response went beyond a ritual and into a mission that looked outward. They asked themselves, can we do something that will save one life? One person from thinking twice about taking another drink. They wanted to make some good come from their grief. They turned their loss into a redemptive mission of healing.

Sandy Hook Elementary School

Who will ever forget December 14, 2012, in Newtown Connecticut and Sandy Hook Elementary School? After fatally shooting his mother, twenty-year-old Adam Lanza shot his way into the school and with his semi-automatic rifle killed twenty children between six- and seven-years old as well as six adult staff members, before taking his own life. This tragedy is the deadliest mass shooting on school grounds in U.S. history. Rebecca Kowalski, whose son Chase died in this horrific event, said, "I could be in the bottom of a bottle; I could not get out of bed. Or, I could do what's making us heal a little bit every day."[16]

Many of the bereaved from Sandy Hook have chosen to not remain on the sidelines. They continue to grieve their unspeakable losses, but they have also chosen activism over stoicism. Alissa Parker and Michele Gay's daughters were killed. They now travel all over the country giving talks about school safety. In honoring their children, they help others, and in helping others they are helping themselves heal.

Still others are doing work for increased gun safety legislation. Some are doing work in the mental health field. People now are being trained to identify a threat before it becomes too late, in the hopes of preventing this type of senseless killing from ever happening again. The Enduring Connection intention not only honors the life of a loved one, it attempts to make sense of the senseless. Meaning is discovered when we honor a loved one and when we extend their memory through a cause and mission that helps others.

Wes Leonard

Wes Leonard was a star athlete for Fennville Michigan High School. He was a three-year starter in both football and basketball. Everyone liked Wes. He was a good kid, a leader who gained respect from coaches and players. On March 3, 2011, Wes was playing in a basketball game at Fennville. He scored a basket in overtime to give his team a 57-55 win. Just after that, he collapsed to the floor in cardiac arrest. He died two hours later from what would be determined as an undetected enlarged heart. He was only sixteen years old.

By August 2011, a mission was born. Wes's family and friends began raising money for Automated External Defibrillators (AEDs). When used properly and quickly, AEDs can save lives and might have saved the life of Wes Leonard. They started the Wes Leonard Heart Team Foundation, a 501(c)(3) nonprofit organization, that to-date has raised funds for 211 AEDs at various schools, mostly across the state of Michigan. Their mission is to have AEDs available, labeled and maintained, in every facility that offers youth athletics.

Wes's life was cut short way too soon, but out of this heartbreaking story was born a mission sure to help others… a mission that reaches outward… that gives meaning to a young man's life and his death.

Stride for Seminarians

On July 14, 2013, six-year-old Gabrielle, ten-year-old Adrianna and eleven-year-old Alexander were tubing on Sylvan Lake in Michigan when a boat struck them. Alexander and Gabrielle died from blunt force trauma, while Adrianna suffered severe injuries but survived. Their father was driving the boat pulling the tube. The driver of the other boat never saw the children.

In 2016, Sandy and I had the honor of meeting the children's parents, John and Ann, at a workshop they invited us to facilitate. They are amazing, faith-filled Christians who are trying every day to persevere in the wake of this tragedy. During this time of grief, they were supported in prayer and community outreach by their Chaldean Church, priests and laypeople alike.

John and Ann wanted to do something to honor their children as well as to show their support for those who helped them during this time and to this day. So about one year after this accident, John and Ann established the *Stride for Seminarians Walk*. It costs over $30,000 for education, room and board for each seminarian at Sacred Heart Seminary in Detroit. Stride for Seminarians holds an annual walk in the Detroit Zoo. Over 1,000 people attend each year and they raise enough money to send two to three seminarians to school where they are formed into tomorrow's leaders of the church.

Here again, a mission that connects lost loved ones with a community of people, working towards a greater purpose to help others, is how this family has chosen to stride forward, looking to heal their wounds, while helping others, one day at a time.

Below are examples of how you can have an Enduring Connection with your loved ones. Remember, whatever you decide to do, you are doing this to not just honor your loved one, which is wonderful, but this intention projects outward beyond a ceremony, towards a mission, large or small, that helps someone else. The good Samaritan cannot be a good Samaritan without the help of another character in the story. Be that Good Samaritan and find someone else to help you complete the story. Be open to God's grace and how He will use your pain to help others.

- Endowments: Give money in your loved one's honor to a cause or non-profit that fits the narrative of their life's story. Try to commit to a multi-year project that fits your budget.

- Scholarships: Award a scholarship named after your loved one to will help someone else attend a private school or university.

- Church: Give money to your church that helps them in their fundraising efforts and special projects.

- Sponsorships: Sponsor someone who is trying to raise money for a cause such as breast cancer or Alzheimer's research.

- Almsgiving: Choose your favorite charity and donate in your loved one's name. Maybe donate some of their clothes or other items to the Salvation Army or Purple Heart. Books could be donated to a public library or church library.

- Plant a tree in your loved one's name. A flowering tree that blooms each spring could be a place where family and friends gather and share memories and stories. The tree will bloom and be a source of beauty for others.

- Buy a park bench and put your loved one's name on it.

- Buy a gift your loved one would approve of for someone else at Christmas.

- Donate your time and become a volunteer at your church, hospital, school or hospice.

- Spend one hour a week in Holy Hour of Adoration, praying for others and your loved one.

- Develop a Facebook page where friends and family can share stories, thoughts and prayers.

- Complete a project that *they* started—maybe an ancestry chart. This is especially true if your loved one was a spouse or parent. You'd be surprised with whom they and/or you might be related. And you'll find new descendants to pray for, who to this point may have had no one to pray for them.

Summary

This intention is mission oriented and thus it has an outward path. It's about taking something bad and making something good, something meaningful come from it. "Gross injustice demonstrates a basic premise, in our world, something is terribly wrong and cries out to be put right."[17] With this intention we are open to God's grace, to what He might do with the pain we feel. The cross was not a symbol, it was used by God to redeem the world. And since God became man to suffer and die for our sins, we are now given the opportunity to share in this redemption. To save the world, one soul at a time, for it is in giving that that we receive. An Enduring Connection extends the bonds of love beyond our deceased loved one and into the arms of others who need our help. In this sense, we are called to be Redemptive Mourners. In helping others, we help ourselves.

The fruit of Christ's sacrifice became our profit; with this intention we sacrifice some of our profits to bear fruit in His Kingdom.

PERSONAL

Questions to reflect on:

What is the best way for you to have an enduring connection with your loved one?

Describe how you can become a Redemptive Mourner.

How can you bring good from bad?

Works of Mercy: Clothe the Naked
Donate used clothing to Purple Heart or The Salvation Army. Do this in honor of your loved one.

Take some quiet time to write...

Your Fifth Intention:
Enduring Connection

It is my intention to...

NOTES

1. Mitch Albom, *Tuesdays with Morrie.* (Anchor Books, 2002).
2. Erasmo Leiva-Merikakis, *Fire of Mercy, Heart of the Word.* (Ignatius Press, 1996).
3. Maria Popova, *Viktor Frankl on the Human Search for Meaning*, Brain Pickings, 2013.
4. Robert A. Neimeyer, *Grief Therapy and the Reconstruction of Meaning: From Principles to Practice.* (Springer Science+Business Media, LLC, 2009). http://www.trauma-ptsd.com/uploads/library/gt_practice_j_contemp_psyc.pdf.
5. Gordon W. Allport, in the Preface to *Man's Search for Meaning*, Viktor E. Frankl, (Boston, Mass.: Beacon Press).
6. Pope Benedict XVI, "Suffering and Love." *God and the World.* (San Francisco, Calif.: Ignatius Press, 2002).
7. Attributed to Léon Bloy, *GoodReads.com.* https://www.goodreads.com/quotes/8319180-the-only-real-sadness-the-only-real-failure-the-only.
8. Fr. Raniero Cantalamessa, Homily, 2007.
9. St. Pope John Paul II, *Salvifici Doloris*, §19.
10. Richard Rohr, *What the Mystics Know.*
11. Martin Luther King, Jr., Speech, "Beyond Vietnam" New York, 4 April 1967.
12. Fr. Thomas Merton, Meditation, Magnificat, August 2018.
13. Pope Benedict XVI. *Jesus of Nazareth.* (San Francisco, Calif.: Ignatius Press, 2007).
14. Fr. John A. Hardon S.J., "John Paul II and the Meaning of Suffering," The Real Presence Association, *The Catholic Faith*, Vol. 8, No. 2. March/April 2002. http://www.therealpresence.org/archives/Martyrs/Martyrs_006.htm, accessed 26 October 2018.
15. St. Pope John Paul II, Speech in Poland, 1979.
16. "Activism, Charity, Sustains Sandy Hook Families Five Years Later." *WKRN. com.* 14 December 2017. https://www.wkrn.com/news/activism-charity-sustain-sandy-hook-families-5-years-later/1077115621.
17. Fleming Rutledge, *The Crucifixion: Understanding the Death of Jesus Christ.* (Grand Rapids, Mich.: Wm. B. Eerdmans Publishing Company, 2017).

 CARYLL HOUSELANDER

Because Christ is in us, any suffering of ours is His passion. He took all human suffering, great and small, and wed Himself to it, crowned it with His crown of thorns, clothed it in His purple garment, gave it the power of His love.

CHAPTER 8

The Sixth Intention: Redefine and Rebuild

PRAYERFUL

And He called the Twelve together and gave them power and authority over all demons and to cure diseases, and He sent them out to preach the kingdom of God and to heal. (LUKE 9:1-2)

Let us pray. *In the name of the Father, and of the son and the Holy Spirit.*

Our mother of sorrows, with strength from above, you stood by the cross, sharing in the sufferings of Jesus, and with tender care you bore Him in your arms, mourning and weeping. We praise you for your faith, which accepted the life planned for you. We praise you for your hope, which trusted that God would do great things in you. We praise for your love in bearing Jesus the sorrows of His passion. Holy Mary, may we follow your example, and stand by all your children who need comfort and love. Mother of God, stand by us in our trials and care for us in our many needs. Pray for us now and at the hour of our death. Amen.

Elizabeth Ann Seton, pray for us.

On another occasion he began to teach by the sea. A very large crowd gathered around him so that he got into a boat on the sea and sat down. And the whole crowd was beside the sea on land. And he taught them at length in parables, and in the course of his instruction he said to them, "Hear this! A sower went out to sow. And as he sowed, some seed fell on the path, and the birds came and ate it up. Other seed fell on rocky ground where it had little soil. It sprang up at once because the soil was not deep. And when the sun rose, it was scorched and it withered for lack of roots. Some seed fell among thorns, and the thorns grew up and choked it and it produced no grain. And some seed fell on rich soil and produced fruit. It came up and grew and yielded thirty, sixty, and a hundred-fold." He added, "Whoever has ears to hear ought to hear." (MARK 4:1-9)

PRACTICAL

T he death of a loved one has a lasting impact and long-term consequences that continue for a lifetime. Even before we might be ready to redefine who we are, culture does it for us. If we lose our only surviving parent, we are orphaned. If our wife dies, we are a widower. If our husband dies, we are a widow. If we are raising children when our spouse dies, (as Sandy and I each were) we are not a "single parent," but an "only parent." Sadly, there is not even a term for the death of a child.

The sixth intention takes a slightly different turn. This intention looks at redefining who we are *apart* from our loved one. Now that our life has changed, what are our new roles? What are our new priorities? What are our new goals, hopes and dreams? How do we go forward with a meaningful life? How can we be more, despite having less?

Assumptive World

We are social people with a primitive need to love and be loved. We are born needing to be loved and cared for just to survive. Loving others is what gives our life meaning and purpose. "Love one another with brotherly affection; outdo one another in showing honor." (Rom 12:10). When death separates our attachment to someone we love, our love for them endures death and we search in vain for something that is now gone. We search in vain for a part of ourselves that is lost. Even after coming to terms with what is lost, we still miss someone. They are not where we want them to be, sitting next to us, enjoying a cup of coffee, talking about decisions, big and small. So, it is only natural to assume that powerful reactions to this loss will follow. This is the very nature of grief. Longing for something we can no longer have leaves us with a broken heart.

> **REDEFINE AND REBUILD**
>
> Redefining and rebuilding our lives looks outward, at life apart from our loved one. What are our new roles and priorities? What are our new hopes, dreams and plans? What is our new relationship with the world?

Our assumptive world precedes loss and is a set of core beliefs, an organized representation of the world we know. It is fundamentally the lens through which we view our world. If we grew up in poverty, we may look at the world through the lens of scarcity, the world we know is lacking, it needs more. Conversely, if we grew up in wealth, we may look at the world through the lens of abundance, the world has plenty of what we need. In watching a documentary of Robert F. Kennedy, he grew up in tremendous wealth, he lacked for nothing. But while Senator of New York, he visited incredible poverty in Appalachia. He was stunned to witness, that a country of such abundance, had places where young children had distended stomachs and were starving to death. His assumptive world suddenly changed. Our beliefs therefore are shaped and reshaped by our life's experiences.

September 11, 2001, might be the greatest example of an assumptive worldview that was changed in an instant. The possibility of multiple airplanes being hijacked by terrorists, rerouted, and set on new suicidal paths to crash into multiple buildings, all within minutes of each other was unthought of—at least by most of us. Yet it happened. Since then boarding an airplane is not the same. Wars were started and have not ended. Many now cast suspicious looks upon people and even luggage. "If you see something, say something" is now part of our lexicon. Life as we had known it changed that day. It will never be the same. We will never look at a skyscraper in the same way. We will never again assume that a plane could not be used as a guided missile that could kill thousands of innocent people.

Many of us may have an assumptive worldview that is kind and loving. That things make sense. We know how we fit into the world. The world is good, even if bad things happen. Others view the world more cautiously. The world is malevolent. As witness to this is the twentieth century and the millions of people who were killed in wars, genocides and holocausts. But no matter what our assumptive worldview is, it tends to change and become corrupted when death strikes close to us, when someone we love dies. Our navigational system gets thrown off course. If our world seemed kind and loving, now suddenly it no longer does. It seems mean and meaningless. It's not a safe place, it's a violent place. Negative assumptions overwhelm us and deprive us from living in the safe comfortable world that we once knew. The world in which we once thought, maybe naively, that we had all the answers, becomes a world in which we question whether we have any answers at all.

This might be especially, but not exclusively, true if our world was rocked by a sudden and violent death of a loved, like suicide, homicide or accident. But many other factors can stun our assumptive world. For instance, what age were we when we grieved our first major death? Who was this person whom we grieved? How did they die?

Once our assumptive world has been inextricably changed by the death of a loved one, there is no re-entry into the old world with the old set of beliefs. That world dissolved. There must be a gradual admission into a new world, with a new worldview, where we learn to be more despite having less. Where we learn to flourish again.

Where we learn to create new identities and new daily patterns of living.

Secondary Losses

At Collin and Kim's wedding in 2012, during the daddy-daughter dance, Sandy looked over and saw Morgan crying her eyes out. She was thinking of her father and her wedding and how he wouldn't be there to dance this dance with her. In that moment, she was not only grieving the loss of her father, she was grieving the loss of something she couldn't have, a dance.

The primary loss is the death of our loved one. But from this loss emerges many secondary or symbolic losses that are attached to the primary loss. When someone whom we love dies, we feel in a sense that we have lost a part of ourselves because we were so connected to our loved one. There is a loss of identity. If our spouse died, our role of husband and wife is no longer. There could be loss of income, loss of financial security and loss of our routine in which our loved one was very much a part.

Secondary losses also entail loss of future hopes, dreams and plans that are no longer viable after our loved one dies. These secondary losses are grieved in the present, for the hopes and dreams planned for in the future. For example, the surviving spouse might grieve in the present the hope he or she had of having children—or more children—in the future. The list of secondary losses is almost endless. Secondary loss is different from the primary loss but are nonetheless real and must be acknowledged and grieved.

With the death of a spouse, the secondary losses are the things that the surviving spouse will have to endure without his or her deceased wife or husband:

- The hope of having children or having additional children;
- The plans of watching children grow up;
- The dreams of children's key milestones, such as graduations, weddings, and career choices;
- The struggle to raise children alone;
- The hope of spending time with grandchildren;
- Retirement and travel plans, growing old together;

- Loss of income and/or financial security;
- Loss of identity as wife or husband;
- The shared rituals, time together;
- The loss of being a wife or husband.

Secondary losses with the death of a child might be:

- Watching this child grow and reach their potential;
- Seeing the fruits of parenting together;
- Parenting a young child into adulthood;
- Key milestone events, graduations, weddings etc.;
- Shared rituals and time together through activities;
- Playing with their future children.

Relearning the World

We all have patterns to our lives. These patterns become habits, and to a large degree become who we are. These patterns are established in part by how we were raised, the genes that we inherited and then our individual preferences as we develop, and grow into our social, occupational and spiritual worlds. Perhaps we attend morning Mass before going to work. Go to lunch at our favorite diner. Stop off at the gym before going home for dinner. Watch some television before going to bed. The next day, the pattern repeats itself. This is not to say that we don't discard some patterns and turn them into new ones. But patterns largely become our life histories. And to a large degree, as we fixate on them, we take them for granted as if they will always be.

Death of a loved one has a way of irrevocably changing these patterns, unwinding them and throwing our world onto an unknown axis where it tends to spin out of control. And as we grieve, we struggle to reestablish a pattern to our new world. We are unfamiliar with this new burgeoning form, because our habits were gripped firmly to the old one. We want that one back. It is beyond our reach.

> At first, I was very afraid of going to places where H. and I had been happy—our favorite pub, or favorite wood. But I decided to do it at once—like sending

a pilot up again as soon as possible after he's had a crash. Unexpectedly, it makes no difference. Her absence is no more emphatic in those places than anywhere else. It's not local at all. The act of living is different all through. Her absence is like the sky, spread over everything.[1]

From his book, *How We Grieve*,[2] Thomas Attig believes that there are primarily five things we must relearn as part of transitioning into our new world while mourning the old one. Remember, part of the mourning process involves looking back on cherished memories, while another part involves looking forward and shaping a new and different life. While we mourn, we must gradually transform old habits and reshape them into new behaviors.

1. **Relearn Physical Surroundings:** This is perhaps the most obvious; it involves the memories we have of our loved one in the environments in which we shared our experiences. This list is not all-encompassing and will be different depending on who we are grieving, but could include, for example: the home, the room in the house where we spent the most time, a bedroom, their place at the dinner table, the favorite restaurant, social gatherings at friends' homes, vacation spots, a car, or church. At first our loss follows us wherever we go and whenever we are. "When our loved one dies, the loss follows us from room to room to room, moment to moment. It is both permanent and ever present."[3] Reactions will be different for everyone. Some of these places can be postponed or avoided, but at some point, we must go home and deal with the cold reality that someone is missing. For some of us, honoring and returning to these places might be a source of comfort where they feel close to the person who died, while for others, seeing an empty place at the dinner table will be a source of great sadness.

The physical surroundings also involve the decisions that need to be made about the belongings of our loved ones. These too will be different, depending on who died.

All these situations are examples of symbolic or secondary losses that must be grieved: the home we live in will never be the same; our child's bedroom that our son or daughter will never again sleep in; our favorite restaurant where we'll never again dine together. We must face these surroundings and eventually even honor them in our own way, yet we can do this in a deliberate way. Nothing needs to be done today that we might regret tomorrow.

2. **Relearn relationships with the living:** Death has a way of revealing things and opening old wounds. Everyone experiences grief in their own unique way. Sometimes these relationships are challenged in ways that we cannot predict.

3. **Relearn Our Selves:** The death of a close loved one changes everything. Our identity, at least in some sense was tied to this person either through blood relationship, legal relationship or close friendship. This loss creates a void in our life, a space of time that was once filled with something and someone, that must now find a new home. Here too, we might need to develop practical new skills as we step into new roles. If our spouse paid all the bill, the bills still must be paid by someone.

4. **Relearn Places in Space and Time:** This involves relearning and adjusting to the important dates on the calendar that will evoke memories and hopes, such as birthdays, an anniversary, annual vacations and holidays.

5. **Relearn our place in the Spiritual World:** For some, Faith is comforting during grief, for others, death of a loved one can at least temporarily dislodge one's relationship with God.

Transformational Resilience

When we think of resilience, it conjures up sentiments of quick recovery from adversity, rising above hardships, fighting through uncertainty and perseverance over the struggles and stresses in life. In the sports world, resilience would mean that a team recovers from a loss, so that they can move on, put the loss behind them and win the next game. If the team focused on losing they'll have a hard time focusing on winning, but they are resilient and strong when they put the past in the rearview mirror and rise to the next challenge, the next opponent.

There is no question, resilience has its place in the world. Resilience is a coping skill that we all need and we all possess in varying levels. Going back to Dr. Davidson's study, the degree to which we are resilient depends on our genes and the environment in which we were raised. Those of us who recover from adversity quickly have a higher level of this skill. Those who get stuck when struggles strike have a lower level.

Grief is not something from which we "recover"; it is something we learn to live with, and even learn from. It is not something we should force into quickly, it's not a race to be won; it's a journey to be lived. Resilience is about "recovering" from a setback and pushing forward anyway. Transformational Resilience is about "discovering" many things, such who we lost, who we now are, and who we want to be. This is not because of a setback, but because of a course correction, a life changing experience. We don't recover our way there, we fumble our way down the path holding on to every branch we can find. But we keep walking, we keep moving forward. With resilience we sharpen our saws to cut through the thicket. We change the path we are on. With transformational resilience we change ourselves and find a new path. We build our bridge on a new road, and a new life awaits us.

We have found through our many workshops that grieving people generally do have a transformative experience. They don't make it back to where they were, they make it forward to where they are. By allowing themselves to be submerged in their pain, grievers give themselves the opportunity to be buoyant again, to bounce back up, to face their future with courage and hope.

Summary

As we come to terms with how our life has changed and we relearn our relationship with our new world, we will at some point begin to look outward and forward to begin to shape our new life. None of this is easy. It is a series of small steps as we look to new hopes, dreams and plans. Some we will realize, some we won't. Take all of this to prayer.

PERSONAL

Questions to reflect on:

Describe... how has your assumptive world been changed?

Name two or three secondary losses of yours.

How will you go about relearning yourself and the world?

Works of Mercy: Feed the Hungry

Consider giving your time, talent and/or treasure to helping the poor. Do this to honor your loved one.

Take some quiet time to write...

Your Sixth Intention: Redefine and Rebuild

It is my intention to...

NOTES

1. C. S. Lewis, *A Grief Observed*. (Harper One, 1961).
2. Thomas Attig, *How We Grieve*. (Oxford University Press, 2011).
3. Steven C. Hayes, Ph.D., "From Loss to Love," *Psychology Today*, July 2018. https://www.psychologytoday.com/us/articles/201806/loss-love, accessed 26 October 2018.

 ST. POPE JOHN PAUL II

Do good by your suffering and do good to those who suffer.

CHAPTER 9

The Seventh Intention: Give and Receive Support

PRAYERFUL

"Go and do likewise." (LUKE 10:37)

Let us pray. *In the name of the Father, and of the Son and the Holy Spirit.*

*God our Father, you have called us
to be witnesses to Jesus
and have commissioned us to lead
all people to encounter him.*

*Send your Holy Spirit
to enlighten our minds
so that your will may be clear to us
and that we may accept it.*

*Dwell within our souls
and make our hearts your own.*

*Transform us into a band of
joyful missionary disciples
embracing the fruits of Synod 16
so as to share the good news
of Jesus Christ in our community
through joyful evangelization and service.*

Come, Holy Spirit,
fill the hearts of your faithful,
and kindle in them the fire of your love. Amen.

Elizabeth Ann Seton, pray for us.

The Parable of the Good Samaritan

But he, desiring to justify himself, said to Jesus, "and who is my neighbor?" Jesus replied, "A man was going down from Jerusalem to Jericho, and fell among robbers, who stripped him and beat him, and departed, leaving him half dead. Now by chance a priest was going down that road; and when he saw him he passed by on the other side. So likewise, a Levite, when he came to the place and saw him, he passed by on the other side.

But a Samaritan, as he journeyed, came to where he was; and he saw him, he had compassion, and went to him and bound his wounds, pouring on oil and wine; then he set him on his own beast and brought him to an inn and took care of him. And the next day he took out two denarii and gave them to the innkeeper, saying 'take care of him; and whatever more you spend, I will repay you when I come back.'

Which of these three do you think, proved neighbor to the man who fell among the robbers?" He said, "The one who showed mercy on him." And Jesus said to him, "Go and do likewise." (LUKE 10:29-37)

PRACTICAL

H ealing comes in small, often unnoticeable and unmeasur-
able increments. One day we look back and realize that
we have traveled a long way from ground zero. We may
not remember the roads we took, the path we made or the bridge
we built that led us to a new and different life, but one thing we do
know—we didn't do any of this in a vacuum. We didn't do any of this
alone. We had help along the way.

The seventh and final intention of mourning is to Give and Receive
Support. When grief is socially supported and validated, it can be
publicly mourned.

One of the greatest benefits of the *Grieving with Great Hope* workshops are the small Grief Peer Groups, where people of a similar
age and loss come together and share stories of their loved ones,
how they died, the life they lived and who they were. Narrative storytelling is part of the healing process because it gives validation by
someone. Simple validation gives us a sense that we are not alone,
and that even though it may feel as though we are going crazy, we are
not—we are grieving.

What Sandy and I notice at
every workshop is the transformation that takes place from
week to week. We often talk
about using a decibel meter to
record the increased sound level from week two to week four
or even from Friday night to
Saturday when on a weekend
workshop. It's very noticeable.

> **GIVE AND RECEIVE
> SUPPORT**
>
> Grief is best when it is socially
> supported, then publicly mourn-
> ed. In giving help to others, we
> become disciples of hope. In
> receiving help from others, we
> recognize the Body of Christ.

The expressions on the faces of the participants change as well. We
see more smiles, more laughs, sprinkled in between some tears.

> I smiled for first time this week. John mentioned
> Friday night that we might even smile tomorrow. I
> thought, "not me." (Phyllis Dwyer)

Sequoia Trees

I have never had the opportunity to stand next to a giant sequoia tree
and stare upward in awe of its majestic beauty. They are believed to

be the largest living organisms on earth. The tallest is 310 feet tall. Many of these trees predate the birth of Christ. They only grow in the Sierra Nevada Mountain range in California and they never grow alone. The giant sequoia tree has a root system that is only 12-15 feet deep. To give some perspective, a tall skyscraper can have a foundation that's 150 feet deep or more. But the sequoia tree doesn't need that because it wraps its roots around the roots of other sequoia trees. These roots can spread for over an acre each. All these roots, wrapped around each other, provide for firm support to withstand the elements that come their way. From *Psychology Today*, "If you want to go it alone, expect to fail alone." Sequoia trees live for thousands of years because they have each other. They are never alone. They share their root systems with each other. They cooperate with each other so that each other can live. They are many, but they are one.

An ant colony has a similar devotion to the common good. There are never any civil wars with ants, no haggling, no drama. They have an inborn need to cooperate with one another. To work towards a common goal.

As the Church Militant, isn't that what we are called to do? To cooperate with one another. To care for one another. To support one another through the hardships in life. To love one another. "Behold, I stand at your door and knock. If anyone hears my voice and opens the door, then I will enter his house and dine with him and he with me" (Rev 3:20). Are we not called to knock on each other's door, to enter their house and break bread with them?

Compassion

When we are in community with one another, like the giant sequoia trees, we share our root systems, and what flows through these root systems is the nourishment of compassion, selflessness and charity. Compassion is aroused by suffering. It is an emotional response to suffering and is an authentic desire to help someone who is suffering. In compassion, we suffer with the sufferer, we are called to their side. We have an innate sense to be compassionate because it is essential for our survival. Whereas depression and anxiety have a "*self*-focus," compassion has an outward "*other*-focus." It is this outward other-focus that lifts not only *our* mood, but also the mood of *others*.

Compassion and empathy are similar; empathy is the emotional experience, the sense of feeling the pain of someone else. With empathy, we might tear up when we feel someone else's pain. When we are compassionate, we have not only a sense for someone's suffering, we want to do something about it. We want to give of ourselves to another. Compassion then can be thought of as the combination of empathy and altruism.

"In all things I have shown you that by toiling one must help the weak, remembering the words of the Lord Jesus, how he said, 'It is more blessed to give than to receive'" (Acts 20:35). Indeed this is true. In a study done at the University of British Columbia, participants received a sum of money. Half were instructed to spend the money on themselves. The other half were told to spend the money on others. At the end of the experiment, the participants who spent the money on others were significantly happier than those who spend the money on themselves.[1]

The Good Samaritan

The message in the parable of the Good Samaritan is at the heart of what it means to be a Christian. Jesus commands us to "Go and do likewise." He calls us to love. To show mercy. To support our fellow neighbor. To be disciples of hope to the hopeless. To help someone else carry their cross, like Simon, even if reluctantly, helped Christ to carry His. "For I have given you an example, that you should do as I have done to you" (John 13:15).

I wrote that during Ann's illness there were "scorekeepers" and "gamers." The scorekeepers would call every now and then to see what the score was, or in other words, how Ann was doing. The scorekeepers watched the game from the last seat in the stadium, or maybe even the Goodyear Blimp. Their absence was noticeable. The gamers would stop by; they got involved in the game. They walked the sidelines and stood in the huddle. They brought a meal, they talked with Ann, they prayed with Ann, they took her for a ride somewhere, anywhere. The "gamers" cared about Ann. The "gamers" were the Good Samaritan, who stopped by the side of the road, not to help a stranger, but to be with an old friend who was dying. To listen to her pain. To support her along the journey. To help her carry her cross until the very end.

When we are grieving, we need Good Samaritans to stop and help us. But we must also take note, and one day turn around and become the Good Samaritan to others.

The Myths of Grief

Grief today is viewed with impatience and misunderstanding. Let's explore some of the myths surrounding grief. Understanding these myths will help us to navigate our path toward healing.

- *Grief is a predictable process that comes in stages.* There are common reactions to grief, such as anger and sadness, but we all experience grief differently, because we are all unique—as is our loss. Also, suggesting that grief is predictable makes it sound passive, which it is not.

- *All loss is the same.* All loss is difficult; no loss is the same. It is best not to compare losses. Grieving a completed suicide will be different than grieving a 95-year-old grandmother. Both however, will have their own set of unique challenges that must be mourned.

- *Grieving is best done alone.* Grief is best when it is socially acknowledged and publicly supported. There are times when being alone can be helpful, yet when we are grieving it better to be with people who will listen to us and help us to process our grief.

- *Keeping busy will take my mind off my pain.* Activity related to healing is fine, for example, writing in a grief journal or going for long walks on a sunny day. However, if keeping busy is used as an avoidance coping strategy, it will only delay the necessary choices that we need to make to begin the mourning process.

- *Tears are sign of weakness.* Unfortunately in our culture today, young boys are socialized to neither cry nor show emotions. Yet Jesus wept. St. Augustine wrote of his tears after his mother St. Monica died. Tears can be both healing and therapeutic; they release toxins from our body. Crying is natural and even helpful.

- *Grieving is a sickness.* Grief is a normal, natural reaction to loss.

The Things People Say at Funerals

What people tell us about our grief can be challenging, sometimes disheartening, often confusing, possibly disenfranchising, and almost always at the most inopportune time. People mean well; some just don't know what to say. Some people think that their bromides will make us feel better, yet maybe what they say is designed to make *them* feel better, more than it is us.

We teach people how to treat us. Without any deference to what is said, people will go on saying the same things only at different funerals and getting the same reactions, from different people. Here are a few of the common things people say, many of which we have heard from participants from a workshop; in great charity a suggested response is included.

- *"I know how you feel."* No one knows how someone else feels. Sometimes a grieving person doesn't even know how they feel. *"With all due respect, I'm not sure I know how I feel. I'm having a difficult time right now, please pray for me."*

- *"He is in a better place now."* This minimizes the loss. He might be in heaven and we pray he is, but right now, we don't know where he is. Faith does not prevent us from the realities of pain. We still miss someone when they die, and it hurts. *"I hope and pray you are right. But I don't know where he is now, and I miss him terribly. Please pray for him and me."*

- *"She would want you to be happy."* Happiness is dependent on circumstances; right now the circumstances make it difficult to be happy. *"I want to feel happy too, but right now I feel sad. Please pray for me."*

- *"You need to move on."* Someone might misinterpret this to mean they should forget about what happened. We will move forward, but please don't rush the process. *"Right now, I don't even know what that means. But thank you for your concern. Please pray for me."*

- *"You'll get over this soon."* We get over a cold. We don't get over grief. We learn, by the Grace of God, to get through it. *"This isn't something I'll get over, but with God's grace and the support from family and friends, I hope to heal one day. Please pray for me."*

- *"God needed another angel."* God doesn't need anything. He has everything that He needs. *"I know you are trying to be helpful. Please pray for me."*

- *"Thank goodness you have other children."* This needs no further narrative. *"I love all my children, here and in heaven. But right now, I'm trying to deal with my baby who just died. Please pray for her and my family."*

What is the correct response we should give to someone who has lost a loved one? No large platitudes are needed, what is best is a simple, *I'm sorry*. Some people might like a warm hug or a hand to hold. Even a smile to look at. If we are close with this person and if we are to be a Disciple of Hope, we should extend an offer to help support them. Often, the only thing that a grieving person wants is a compassionate ear. Compassionate listening is listening without judging, analyzing, criticizing or comparing. We listen to understand and show concern. We give the person we are listening to the center stage in our brain. It's as though we are playing tennis, but we never serve, they and only they serve. We simply return volley, softly to their side of the court.

"Could I come by sometime next week with dinner or lunch? If you like, I'd love to let you talk. What day is good for you?"

Hole of the Flute

An African proverb says, "If you want to go quickly, go alone. If you want to go far, go together." Studies show us that during the first year of grief, sometimes up to 90% of our healing community can change. Friends become strangers and strangers become friends. Some of our friends (or former friends) simply don't know what to do when trouble strikes. We love them anyway, yet we seek help from those who are willing and able to offer it.

I love this passage from Luke's gospel, "For figs are not gathered from thorns, nor grapes picked from a bramble bush" (LUKE 6:44). Jesus goes on to say that a good man produces good and an evil man produces evil. All true; yet I like this passage because how it speaks to me in another way. We all have gifts. I am not a good plumber, so I wouldn't be good at fixing a leaky pipe. Yet I'd like to think that I could sit and listen to someone, to console and support them. I like what Fr. Richard Rohr says, "Sometimes we are simply called to be present to them and to be Jesus to them."[2]

> "I am the hole of the flute that the Christ's breath
> moves through… My role as a chaplain is to be open
> and to accept. To be open to God and to others, and
> to accept whatever comes in. I don't make the music
> or control it. I simply open myself up and accept the
> breath of life, the holy spirit of God. I am the hole of
> the flute, listen to this music."[3]

Sandy and I often say that we are holes in the flute. We simply let
the Holy Spirit supply the air that makes the music. Sometimes all it
takes to help someone through sorrow is to sit and be still with them,
be present, listen to their story, be a hole in the flute, let God do the
rest. All of us should be able to do that.

Disciples of Hope

I have used the term "Disciple of Hope" several times in this book,
without explaining what it means. In the Christian meaning, a disciple is a dedicated follower of Jesus Christ. What did Jesus do in
His ministry? He healed people: the lepers, the blind, the lame, the
hungry, the sinners, the outcasts, even the dead. He touched hearts.
He taught us how to love and how to pray. Jesus also taught us how
to mourn. After His friend Lazarus died, Jesus wept. He expressed
sadness in the form of tears.

The goal of this ministry is to begin to send forth more and more
people who have been through their grief journey—maybe in some
sense are *still* going through it—yet are willing to walk across the
other side of the road, bend a knee and lend an ear to someone who
is going through theirs. A Disciple of Hope is not only actively involved in their own healing, but when the time is right, gets actively
involved in supporting others, in helping others to heal their wounds.
They have mercy on others. They extend mercy to others.

Ask yourself this question: Are you willing to go and do likewise?

> "Just as each of us has one body with many members,
> and these members do not all have the same func-
> tion, so in Christ we who are many form one body,
> and each member belongs to all the others. We have

different gifts, according to the grace given us. If a man's gift is prophesying, let him use it in proportion to his faith. If it is serving, let him serve; if it is teaching, let him teach; if it is encouraging, let him encourage; if it is contributing to the needs of others, let him give generously; if it is leadership, let him govern diligently; if it is showing mercy, let him do it cheerfully" (Rom 12:4-8).

Summary

It is not a sign of weakness to accept help from someone. Indeed, it takes courage to admit our frailty, to admit that we cannot do this alone. "And let us consider how to stir up one another to love and good works, not neglecting to meet together, as is the habit of some, but encouraging one another, and all the more as you see the day drawing near" (Heb 10:24-25). It is providential to seek and receive support from others who want to help; when the time comes, it will be equally providential to extend help to someone else, to be the Good Samaritan.

PERSONAL

Questions to reflect on:

Who is the first person you call when you need someone to talk to?

To what myth of grief do you most relate?

How do you think you'll know when you are ready to be a Disciple of Hope?

Works of Mercy: Care for Creation
Plant a tree and nourish it.

Take some quiet time to write…

Your Seventh Intention: Give and Receive Support

It is my intention to…

NOTES

1. Association for Psychological Science, The Compassionate Mind. 2013.
2. Richard Rohr, *What the Mystics Know*. (The Crossroad Publishing Company, 2015).
3. Attributed to Hafiz, on *GoodReads.com*.

 ERNEST HEMINGWAY

The world breaks everyone, and afterward, some are strong in the broken places.

Epilogue

"Without a vision, the people perish." (Prov 29:18)

T here is no need to minimize our grief, to push it under the rug, to pretend that it's not there, to wish it away—quickly. Some of our friends, and even family, can often do a pretty good job of that for us. It is up to us then, to broadcast our grief, from the highest hilltop and the lowest valley. Let everyone close to us know; yes, I am grieving; yes, I am hurting; yes, I am sad; and yes, I do miss someone very much. But do you know what? It's okay that I feel this way. It says something about who I am. That I care. That I feel. That I love. That I'm normal. That I am grieving.

We have come a long way, but, where do we go from here?

There are two main points in this closing argument. The first is we need to grieve with hope and then mourn with intention. The second is that grief is a binary path to healing; an inward-looking path and an outward-looking path.

Grieve with Hope

St. Paul writes, "But we should not be ignorant brethren, concerning those who are asleep, that we may not grieve as others who have no hope. For since we believe that Jesus died and rose again, even so, through Jesus, God will bring with him those who have fallen asleep." He ends with, "Therefore comfort one another with these words" (1 Thess 4:13-14, 17).

What is Paul telling us? Those who have fallen asleep is a reference to those who have died before us. He was comforting the living about the dead, that if they died in full faith, God will bring them home. But those who have no faith, are those without hope. Those who don't believe that Christ suffered, died and rose from the dead, are those without our hope, so let us not grieve like them. Hope is not referred to here as wish or a dream or something to which we aspire. It is a confident promise that will one day be fulfilled.

Paul is *not* telling us to not feel, to not grieve. The happiest people are those who enjoy spending time with those they love. When someone we love dies, that time is stripped away from us. How can we not feel that? Paul knew that Jesus grieved. When Jesus' friend Lazarus died, even though He knew that He would soon bring Lazarus out of the tomb, Jesus still felt something; he felt grief. Jesus felt our human emotions because they were His emotions too. Hope does not insulate us from grief, it does not cushion our suffering, but it does give us a confident belief that eternity awaits us, and one day, all will be well again. So, grieve, my goodness grieve, but try as best you can to grieve with great hope.

Mourn with Intention

Grief is a reflexive, instinctive, subconscious reaction. *Mourning* is our learned, intentional and conscious response. Mourning is what we do with how we feel. It is not passive; we are very active when we mourn. Mourning is a coping mechanism that helps us to adapt to a new world into which we have just been thrown without our permission. Mourning is not a task that we can do rather unconsciously, just as we might brush our teeth. Nor does it occur in linear, progressive stages, with a beginning, middle and end. We mourn the rest of our lives, but it should become a transformative experience. Mourning helps us to restore good. Not the way good was, but a new form of good.

Intention is a mental state to bring about a desired goal in the future, based on the belief that our actions will satisfy a desire. It is what we consciously want to experience or create. It involves planning and cognition. What are these goals and desires?

Aristotle believed that happiness is found in a lifetime of doing good, of *giving* more than *receiving*. We know from St. Pope John Paul II that, "Man suffers when he experiences any kind of evil," evil being a lack, limitation or distortion of good. Suffering is then active in our lives when we are deprived or cut off from good. So, if doing good

138 •

brings us happiness, being deprived of good would have an opposite effect—sadness, grief, anguish.

Happiness then is rediscovered when good is restored, through a means that is different than that which previously brought us happiness. The goal then of intention is to embrace our suffering, in such a way that we move away from evil and toward a restored good, in ourselves and others. Mourning is the mechanism in which we restore this good.

For example, an intention for the Fifth Intention of Mourning might read something like this: *"It is my intention to reconstruct my relationship and look outward towards a redemptive mission to help others."* "Reconstruct," "redemptive mission," "help others" are all affirming statements that seek to restore good from bad. But they are only statements at this point. This is only our *intention*. Mourning then is our conscious response. Through an Act of Mercy, an Endowment, giving alms, planting a tree, volunteering, starting a nonprofit we slowly take tangible measures to restore good. Meaning is always found in our response, what we do with the cards we've been dealt. Dr. Allen Frances writes, "The best way to go from misery to happiness is to find a cause you believe in and work hard for it."[1]

What is *your* vision? How will you begin to navigate your path to a new and different life?

The Binary Path to Healing

Grief is not only a reaction to loss, it is also a process in which we heal. And when looking at grief as a process, as was previously discussed, we must consider it to be a twofold track. It is on both paths that we take an active role; we accept complete responsibility for our healing, yet we take small steps along the way. "Nothing happens until something moves."[2]

The inward-looking path is reflective and often emotional. It is on this path that we look back at what *was*, while we come to terms with what *is*—we face our pain. Here are some coping strategies as we journey along this path.

Prayer: Take time to be still every day, maybe 30-60 minutes, preferably in the morning, before you begin your day. Read the daily scripture readings and reflections, ponder what God is trying to tell you. Use this time to be in His presence. Pray for your needs but give thanks as well. Try to spend one hour each week in Eucharistic Adoration at your church. Attend daily Mass as often as you can. Attend a Bible study or Alpha Group at your church.

Rituals and Remembering: Rituals are things you do that help you to have an enduring connection with your loved one. There is an almost boundless list from lighting a candle, to commemorating a park bench, to starting a new holiday tradition. Be creative. Journal your thoughts. Talk to friends and family.

Acceptance: Learning to accept and come to terms with what happened is very important, as is managing thoughts, including the same bad tape that plays over in your brain about how you can't do this and won't do that. You (and most of us) spend 99% of your time on automatic pilot. Become more conscious and intentional. Rumination is not action. Denial is a defense mechanism with a short shelf life.

Emotions and Feelings: You must learn to understand your emotions and manage your feelings. Emotions are instinctual; feelings are expressed in thoughts. Feelings happen to you, yet you have some control over them. Just because someone made you angry, doesn't mean you have to be an angry person. Control your worry, it helps nothing.

Forgiveness: Forgiveness is a process, and a difficult one at that. With forgiveness you choose love over hate, the future over the past.

Gratefulness: Like forgiveness, gratefulness is a choice. Simply searching your brain for things to be grateful for, will change your brain's chemistry by releasing endorphins. Being grateful for the little things in life, even when life isn't going as we planned, is a healthy coping mechanism to practice daily.

The outward-looking path is more collaborative and engaging. Here we look forward to what can be: a future we didn't ask for, but a future we have nonetheless, and a future to which we must learn to adapt. Here we have the opportunity, if we are open to God's grace, to allow our suffering to be redemptive and meaningful. It is here that we become disciples of hope, by reaching beyond ourselves.

Meaning and Purpose: One way to find meaning in your life is through purposeful work. What better way is there to have an enduring connection with your loved ones than to engage in meaningful activities in which they are at the core of why you do what you do?

Redemptive Mission: When you are open to God's grace, you allow Him to take your suffering and make meaning come from it. In this sense it is redemptive, because Christ elevated human suffering to a supernatural level. He gave us all the power to be Good Samaritans to help His Kingdom. Christ wants us to profit from the fruit of his sacrifice, but he wants also to sacrifice our profits, for the fruit of His Kingdom.

Rebuild means relearning the world: Roles change. Friends change. Life is one big change. You are now faced with coming to terms with all of this. Take it slow. Don't make any rash decisions or any major decisions for about twelve months. Consider transformational resilience and the new discoveries that you can make about yourself.

Take Care of YOU: Take long walks. Get a check-up from head to toe. Eat healthier. Meditate. Exercise if you can, and as often as you can. Take naps. Get seven to eight hours of sleep each night.

Get Support and be Supportive: *Accept* that you can't and shouldn't do this alone. Look for supportive friends and family who will listen and validate you. Start your own group. Get together for coffee or a gathering at your house. Talk. Listen. Share.

Let Us Begin

To borrow a quote from John F. Kennedy: "All this will not be finished in the first one hundred days. Nor will it be finished in the first one thousand days... nor even perhaps in our lifetime on this planet. But let us begin."[3]

No truer words could be spoken about grief. All our grief and pain will not be finished in the first one hundred days, nor in the first one thousand days. We will mourn in one form or another for the rest of our lives. So let us begin.

Let us begin to enrich our prayer life and encounter our Lord. *"God did not put me on this earth to be successful, He put me on the earth to be faithful"* (St. Mother Teresa of Calcutta).

Let us begin to be a witness to others on how to mourn. *"Amen, amen, I say to you. You will weep and mourn while the world rejoices, you will grieve, but your grief will become joy"* (John 16:20).

Let us begin to grieve with hope. *"He will wipe away every tear from their eye and there will be no more death or mourning"* (Rev 21:4).

Let us begin with small steps to build our bridge to a new and different life. *"For unless our hearts are broken, how else can God get in?"* (ARCHBISHOP FULTON J. SHEEN).

Let us begin to mourn with intention. *"I have done what is mine to do, now you must do what is yours"* (ST. FRANCIS OF ASSISI).

Let us begin to find meaning from our suffering. *"We give our suffering meaning by the ways we choose to respond to it"* (VIKTOR FRANKL).

Let us begin to live a more purposeful life. *"I want to spend my heaven, doing good on earth"* (ST. THERESE OF LISIEUX).

Let us begin to realize that how we live can honor those we love who have died. *"Every person must love or go crazy because no person is sufficient for himself"* (ARCHBISHOP FULTON J. SHEEN).

Let us begin to be a Disciple of Hope to others. *"If you are what you should be, you will set the world ablaze"* (ST. CATHERINE OF SIENNA).

Let us begin to be a Redemptive Mourner. *"In bringing about redemption through human suffering, Christ raised human suffering to the level of redemption"* (ST. POPE JOHN PAUL II).

Let us begin to do Acts of Mercy in honor of our loved one. *"When we handle the sick and needy, we touch the suffering body of Christ"* (ST. MOTHER TERESA OF CALCUTTA).

Let us begin to find support from those we love. *"In pastoral ministry, we must accompany people, we must heal their wounds"* (POPE FRANCIS).

Let us begin to forgive those whom have transgressed upon us. *"Where sin increased, grace abounded all the more"* (ROM 5:20).

Let us begin to forgive ourselves. *"All our trials and sufferings come from not understanding ourselves"* (ST. TERESA OF AVILA).

Let us begin to be more grateful and see beauty in everything. *"Thanks is the highest form of thought and gratitude is happiness doubled by wonder"* (G.K. CHESTERTON).

Let us begin to be more despite having less. *"I am a hole in the flute, Christ's breath moves through. Listen to the music"* (HAFIZ).

Let us begin to let no suffering go wasted, no pain not be used for the better good.

Let us begin today.

God bless you!

NOTES

1. Dr. Allen Frances, *The Twilight of American Sanity*. (HarperCollins Publishers, 2017).
2. Albert Einstein quoted in Robert Ringer, "Nothing Happens Until Something Moves," *Early to Rise*, (blog). 7 August 2012. https://www.earlytorise.com/nothing-happens-until-something-moves/ accessed 14 November 2018.
3. President John F. Kennedy, *Inaugural Address*. Washington, D.C., 20 January 1961.

 REV 21:1-5

Then I saw a new heaven and a new earth; for the first heaven and the first earth had passed away, and the sea was no more. And I saw the holy city, new Jerusalem, come down out of heaven from God, prepared as a bride adorned for her husband; and I heard a great voice from the throne saying, "Behold, the dwelling of God is with men. He will dwell with them and they shall be his people, and God himself will be with them; he will wipe away every tear from their eyes, and death shall be no more, neither shall there be mourning, not crying nor pain anymore, for the former things have passed away. Behold, I make all things new.

APPENDIX

The Train

The train is a metaphor for life, schedules perfectly timed, a symphony of sorts, things that collide in a rapture of noise and movements, beyond what we know, beyond what we see. A goodbye is somehow met with a hello. When one door closes, another opens, passing in a whisper, without our consent.

The day you arrived on the train changed my life forever. The door opened and there you were. All smiles. Every day after — a gift from God. We sojourned together. So many places. We glowed when loved ones joined us. We lamented when someone departed. We wondered, didn't we, where they went? We never knew. Until now.

What would I change? Not a thing. For to change anything, changes everything. And everything was just as it was supposed to be. With love comes all the good, mixed with meaningful anguish of bad. On the cross we find all our suffering and all our hope.

From the day we met, we knew one of us would slide through that mysterious gate before the other. One of us would be spared from grief, while the other would not. Sorry to say it was me whose time had come to depart the train. The train is a momentary ride for all of us. Its only permanence is that it rolls on even without us.

And so, the train rolls on without me, but not without you. I may not be as close as I was, but I'm not far away. And a piece of me, will always be with you. So, miss me if you will, but honor my life with the way you live yours.

I felt the train slowing down. And when it came to a final stop, somehow, I slipped away from you, and into the arms of others who I had honored. It was as if they knew. They smiled. We laughed. Even Jesus caught my eye and winked, "well done." He said, "good and faithful servant." And I thought, this is why I lived.

So, grieve, but mourn with splendid hope. For hope will not disappoint. Remember me in the great cloud of spectators, cheering for you, cheering for your train to roll on. It was just my time. That is all. Your time will come too. And there I will be. All smiles. Jesus too. Waiting for you to come back to me.

About Good Mourning Ministry

GMM is a Catholic bereavement organization. Guided by the Holy Spirit, we are a resource to Catholic parishes and people who are mourning the loss of a loved one. Our vision is to be bearers of hope. To be transformative in our work, by offering prayerful, practical and personal grief support.

John and Sandy O'Shaughnessy are the co-founders of Good Mourning Ministry. Both experienced the depths of grief and transformation through mourning.

John is a Certified Grief Counselor (GC-C) and published author of his own riveting true story of amazing love, to the dead end of grief and a return to hope. *The Greatest Gift—A Return to Hope* was published in 2007 and took John out of the corporate world into supporting the bereaved. He volunteered and worked for seven years at a non-profit bereavement support organization where he was grief group facilitator, workshop speaker, grant writer, and was on the board of directors for three years. In 2012 John finished his first novel. *Encounter* is a story of a young man's extraordinary encounter, somewhere between this life and the next, with a mother whom he thought he lost forever, yet somehow found again. This is John's fifth book.

Sandy is Director of Religious Education at Our Lady of Good Counsel Parish and holds a master's degree in Pastoral Ministry/Bereavement (MAPM). She feels "called" to minister to those who mourn. Sandy lost her mother in 1999, months after being paralyzed in a car accident. Her husband, David, died a year later. She became an "only parent" to two young children.

Together, John & Sandy have four children: Eric, Collin, Morgan, and Ryan; daughter-in-law Kim, and in 2018 they were blessed to welcome granddaughter Claire into the world. Our Lady of Good Counsel in Plymouth, Michigan is John & Sandy's home parish.

Visit us at: www.goodmourningministry.net
Email us at: goodmourningministry@hotmail.com

Also, from John O'Shaughnessy
The Greatest Gift – A Return to Hope
Encounter – A Novel

From John and Sandy O'Shaughnessy
Grieving with Great Hope
Finding the Words – A Grief Journal

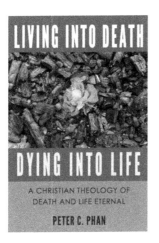

CPSIA information can be obtained
at www.ICGtesting.com
Printed in the USA
BVHW051548250123
657086BV00003B/71